THE ESSENTIAL JACK NICHOLSON

THE ESSENTIAL
JACK NICHOLSON

James L. Neibaur

ROWMAN & LITTLEFIELD
Lanham • Boulder • New York • London

Published by Rowman & Littlefield
A wholly owned subsidary of The Rowman & Littlefield Publishing Group, Inc.
4501 Forbes Boulevard, Suite 200, Lanham, Maryland 20706
www.rowman.com

Unit A, Whitacre Mews, 26-34 Stannary Street, London SE11 4AB

British Library Cataloguing in Publication Information Available

Library of Congress Cataloging-in-Publication Data

Names: Neibaur, James L., 1958– author.
Title: The essential Jack Nicholson / James L. Neibaur.
Description: Lanham : Rowman & Littlefield, 2017. | Includes bibliographical
   references and index. | Includes filmography.
Identifiers: LCCN 2016016385 (print) | LCCN 2016024154 (ebook) | ISBN
   9781442269880 (hardback : alk. paper) | ISBN 9781442269897 (electronic)
Subjects: LCSH: Nicholson, Jack—Criticism and interpretation.
Classification: LCC PN2287.N5 N46 2016 (print) | LCC PN2287.N5 (ebook) | DDC
   791.4302/8092—dc23
LC record available at https://lccn.loc.gov/2016016385

Printed in the United States of America

To my friend Gary Schneeberger.
Thanks for handing me a million laughs.

CONTENTS

ACKNOWLEDGMENTS

Special thanks to Katie Carter, who lives every book with me, film by film, chapter by chapter, and offers valuable insight.

Special thanks to Terri Lynch, who for a decade has pored over my prose and suggested rewrites that made it that much better.

These women are indispensable.

Thanks to Ted Okuda, whose three decades of help on every one of my projects from my very first book has been, and remains, invaluable.

And thanks to Max Neibaur, James Zeruk, Paul Gierucki, Gary Schneeberger, Peter Jackel, John Heckinlively, Steve Johnson, Scott McGee, Turner Classic Movies, the Racine Public Library interlibrary loan, and the Wisconsin Center for Film and Theater Research.

Final thanks must go to Mr. Jack Nicholson himself, whose work inspired this project and who is the greatest actor of his generation.

INTRODUCTION

This is not a complete, comprehensive overview of Jack Nicholson's film career for scholars. This publisher's Essential series is for mainstream movie fans who have a general interest in a performer's work. Thus, we are looking at most of Nicholson's movies, not all of them. While each film will be examined in some depth, we will be focusing on those movies that help define Jack Nicholson's work—be they aesthetically good or bad.

Jack Nicholson started in low-budget Roger Corman films, where he learned as an actor, writer, and director. He was soon up-and-coming talent, rapidly rising to the status of a bona fide movie star and, ultimately, a motion picture icon. His career includes some of the finest films and most celebrated performances in all of movie history. Examining his film career is to explore the evolution of a gifted performer who challenged a lot of conventions and caused us to broaden our definition of a leading man.

Nicholson is rather unique in that he had the starring role in his film debut, Roger Corman's *The Cry Baby Killer* (1958). He spent the early part of his career getting big roles in smaller pictures and small roles in bigger ones, balancing these with appearances in various television programs and doing some stage work. It was Peter Fonda's youth culture drama *Easy Rider* (1969) that was Nicholson's initial breakthrough. Following up with *Five Easy Pieces* (1970) furthered his impact. His Best Actor Oscar nomination for *The Last Detail* (1974) is what elevated Nicholson to full-fledged movie star. The multi-Oscar-winning *One Flew over the Cuckoo's Nest*

(1975) caused him to achieve superstar status. Gradually his superstardom approached the level of cinema icon, and it is there where he remains, even after decelerating and then concluding his motion picture career. Through it all, he enjoyed success as a screenwriter, an actor, and even an animator.

In our study of the essential films of Jack Nicholson, we will not limit our focus to his starring films, his biggest hits, or even on his most critically acclaimed work. While there isn't much to say about many of the smaller supporting roles he played early in his career (*Ensign Pulver* [1964], *The St. Valentine's Day Massacre* [1967]), there is some significance to a few from this period (*The Little Shop of Horrors* [1960], *The Raven* [1963]). Once he was established in *Easy Rider*, his output remained erratic. Nicholson did some films that were not particularly impactful on the advancement of his career (*On a Clear Day You Can See Forever* [1970], *King of Marvin Gardens* [1972]), along with others that did (*Carnal Knowledge* [1971]). Once he established stardom and was rising to icon status, nearly all of his films, good and bad, are worthy of some discussion. However, this does not include cameos in films like *Broadcast News* (1987), *Mars Attacks!* (1996), or *Evening Star* (1996), but does include strong supporting performances in *Reds* (1981) and *A Few Good Men* (1992). The criteria as to what would be considered an essential Jack Nicholson film and deserving of a full-chapter assessment in our study are mostly based on the film's importance to his career. However, because he established himself as an icon during his career, we do get to the point where virtually all of his films are significant in their presentation of that iconic screen persona.

At the time of this writing, Jack Nicholson had not made a film since 2010. Word got out that he retired at seventy-six due to being unable to remember lines as clearly as he once had. However, Nicholson claimed he did not retire; he simply lost interest:

> I'm not going to work until the day I die, that's not why I started this. I mean, I'm not driven. I was driven—but I'm not, I don't have to be out there any more. . . . I had the most chilling thought that maybe people in their twenties and thirties don't actually want to be moved anymore. They may want just to see more bombs, more explosions, because that is what they have grown up with. And I'll never do that type of movie.[1]

Robert Downey Jr. attempted to lure Nicholson out of retirement for his film *The Judge* (2014), but Nicholson refused and the role went to Robert Duvall. Downey also wanted Nicholson for *Sherlock Holmes 3* (2016), but Nicholson stuck to his promise of not wanting to do "that type of movie."[2]

Jack Nicholson's cinematic legacy is quite brilliant, and his quirky characterizations exhibited a consistent versatility as well as a discernible focus that raised the value of even his less interesting projects. As we examine the essential films of this iconic actor's career, we will explore his growth as an actor, his choices and challenges, and his ability to reinvent himself while redefining the concept of the American movie star. He was an actor who could exhibit both edginess and complacence, volatility and tenderness, outrageousness and stoicism—all as ingredients within the same characterization. His twelve Oscar nominations make him the most nominated male actor in the Academy's history. This book examines his cinematic accomplishments.

RATINGS KEY

The "essential" movies selected for this book are rated accordingly, as follows:

Five stars (★★★★★): A classic, not only as a Nicholson film but as a film overall

Four stars (★★★★): A great or near great film that has the essential Nicholson qualities in it and features solid filmmaking

Three stars (★★★): A good film, especially one that had a great Nicholson performance in it

Two stars (★★): An average film; a film worth seeing at least once or a film that one can take or leave, no harm done either way

There are no ratings lower than two stars.

PROLOGUE

Jack Nicholson's Early Life

Jack Nicholson was born to June Frances Nicholson, out of wedlock, on April 22, 1938, in Neptune City, New Jersey. While his mother pursued a career as a showgirl and dancer, Jack was brought up by his maternal grandparents. He was brought up believing his grandparents were his parents, and his mother and aunt were his sisters. It was not until the 1970s that Jack found out the truth about his family. Some biographies indicate he was informed by a *Time* reporter doing a feature story on the actor.[1] Nicholson's scholastic career was both good and bad. While he excelled academically, he was a class clown in school, often getting into trouble. He was in detention every day one school year.[2] Once out of school, Nicholson served a tour of duty in the Air National Guard and then headed to Hollywood, where he could live with relatives and pursue an interest in theater.

Jack Nicholson's first employment in Hollywood was working odd jobs at the MGM cartoon studio, in the offices of William Hanna and Joseph Barbera, who were at that time producing the popular Tom and Jerry and Droopy Dog cartoons. Nicholson had a flair for art and a talent for drawing that impressed the cartoon producers enough to offer him a position as an animator. He turned it down, as he wanted to become an actor or perhaps a screenwriter. Nicholson made some connections while working at MGM, including producer Joe Pasternak, who arranged for him to join Jeff Corey's acting classes. Nicholson would later state that Jeff Corey taught him everything he knew about acting.[3] In an interview with *Film Comment*, Nicholson recalled,

> I hadn't cared about much but sports and girls and looking at movies—stuff you do when you're 17 or 18. But Jeff Corey's method of working opened me up to a whole area of study. Acting is life study and Corey's classes got me into looking at life as—I'm still hesitant to say—an artist. They opened up people, literature. I met Robert Towne, [Carole] Eastman, [John] Shaner, and loads of people I still work with. From that point on, I have mainly been interested in acting. I think it's a great job, a fine way to live your life. Corey taught that good actors were meant to absorb life, and that's what I was trying to do. This was the era of the Beat Generation and West Coast jazz and staying up all night on Venice Beach.[4]

Nicholson soon joined the Players Ring Theater of Los Angeles to further study his craft, and performed in several local plays. His first play was *Tea and Sympathy* for the Players Ring, for which he made only fourteen dollars per week. He supplemented this small income by continuing to work for the MGM animation department. He also landed a role on an NBC drama entitled *Are You Listening*, which was broadcast on September 3, 1956. Nicholson recalled for *Film Comment*,

> I tried to keep my day job during this period but they closed the MGM cartoon department on me. Along with George Bannon, I was its last employee; I remember wrapping up all the drawings for storage. During the interim between jobs, I got a part in a play downtown. At the time, the only professional theaters in L.A. were road companies, but there were a lot of little theaters where you were paid about $20 a week. However, in this theater there were too many seats and it couldn't come under a little-theater contract, so I was paid $75 a week.[5]

It was while he was appearing in a play in Los Angeles that Nicholson was spotted by low-budget movie producer Roger Corman. Corman felt that Jack's lean, attractive looks would be right for his planned production *The Cry Baby Killer*. Jeff Corey recommended Nicholson for the role.

Roger Corman was interested in capitalizing on the young delinquent dramas that had become popular after the success of James Dean's films *East of Eden* (1954) and *Rebel without a Cause* (1955). Another film, *The Blackboard Jungle* (1955), dealt with juvenile troublemakers in an inner-city school, with Bill Haley's "Rock around the Clock" on the soundtrack. The rock-and-roll explosion was in full swing by 1958, and the most recent

Elvis Presley films, *Jailhouse Rock* (1957) and *King Creole* (1958), cast the singer as a tough young man who rebelled against society. Nicholson agreed to star in *The Cry Baby Killer* and prepared to make his theatrical film debut.

THE CRY BABY KILLER

(1958, Allied Artists)

★ ★ ½

Director: Joe Addis
Screenplay: Leo Gordon, Melvin Levy
Producers: David Kramarsky, David March. *Executive Producer:* Roger Corman.
   Cinematographer: Floyd Crosby. *Editor:* Irene Morra
Cast: Jack Nicholson (Jimmy Wallace), Harry Lauter (Police Lt. Porter),
   Carolyn Mitchell (Carole Fields), Brett Halsey, (Manny Cole), Lynn
   Cartwright (Julie), Ralph Reed (Joey), John Shay (Gannon), Barbara
   Knudson (Mrs. Maxton), William Forester (Carl Maxton), John Weed
   (Sgt. Reed), Frank Richards (Pete), Bill Erwin (Wallace), James Filmore
   (Al), Smoki Whitfield (Sam), Ed Nelson (Rick), Mitzi McCall (Evelyn),
   Roger Corman (Joe), Claude Stroud (Werner), Ruth Swanson (Mrs.
   Wallace), Herb Vigran (Lawson), Leo Gordon (bit)
Released: August 17, 1958
Specs: 70 minutes; black and white
Availability: DVD (Buena Vista Home Entertainment/Hollywood Pictures)

Roger Corman was a noted low-budget film producer whose product was
derisively dismissed by critics during its time but has since become lauded
as a quintessential example of maverick filmmaking at its cleverest and most
resourceful. Corman liked to exploit trends, and in *The Cry Baby Killer*, the
trend was the juvenile delinquent drama that became popular in postwar
American movies. James Dean had just made his enormous impact on the

subgenre three years earlier in *Rebel without a Cause*, and his death in September 1955 made him a timeless representation of youthful angst. Elvis Presley's rock-and-roll rebellion lit up the movie screens from 1956 until 1958, when he entered the army. Other films followed suit, realizing the teen audience that was embracing the new rebellious rock-and-roll sound was a ready market for such dramas.

Jack Nicholson has the distinction of playing the lead role—in fact, the title role—in his movie debut. He portrays Jimmy Wallace, a disillusioned, defiant seventeen-year-old. Jimmy is confronted by two young thugs, ordered by a man named Manny Cole to rough him up. Manny has designs on Jimmy's girl, Carole. Jimmy shoots the men in self-defense and believes he killed them, so he panics and flees the scene. Ending up in a storage room at a drive-in, the desperate Jimmy takes the janitor, a young mother, and her baby hostage as police surround him. Meanwhile, spectators at the drive-in find this incident more entertaining than the movie being shown, and their attention is drawn as police and acquaintances try to talk Jimmy into freeing the hostages and giving himself up.

Despite securing the lead in his first movie, Jack Nicholson still made an inauspicious debut in *The Cry Baby Killer*. There are basic rudiments of the talent he would continue to hone throughout the early part of his career, but his performance in his movie debut would never cause someone to conclude that Nicholson would emerge as one of the greatest motion picture icons of his time. The film itself has some promise, with a script that offers some interesting ideas, but too often it relies upon predictable situations and conclusions. Had it not been Nicholson's debut, it would likely have been considered little more than a competent, unremarkable low-budget drama.

Watching it with the knowledge of Nicholson's career trajectory, you can see hints of the kind of crazed character he'd later become most well known for playing. He overacts a great deal in this debut, spending most of the film yelling. Sometimes this comes off as so outrageous that it helps to demonstrate the overactive frustration of the lead character, for example, when he yells at a woman to stop her baby from crying without realizing the futility of such a request. *The Cry Baby Killer* drags at times despite being only an hour long. One can see that the movie is trying to say something about the insensitivity of people and the media, based on the entertainment the onlookers appear to derive from watching the hostage situation escalate, but it doesn't always come off too strongly.

Corman would later claim that *The Cry Baby Killer* is the first of his productions that did not net a profit, although it did eventually manage to earn back its costs. Acting only as executive producer, Corman stated that he was out of the country during preproduction, and the producers changed the script. When he returned just as filming commenced, he attempted to return things that had been cut from the screenplay, but only partially succeeded in doing so. It might have been a different—and better—movie had Corman directed it himself and if Leo Gordon's script had been followed more closely.

The Cry Baby Killer is significant as being Jack Nicholson's film debut, making it essential to an overview of his career, but it is a decidedly unremarkable programmer from Corman's production company and only interesting from a historical perspective. Critics of the period overlooked it, but when it was released to DVD in 2007, the *Sacramento News and Review* stated:

> This low-budget 1958 Roger Corman production is mainly notable as the cinematic debut of 21-year-old Jack Nicholson, who met Corman in an acting class. The future three-time Oscar winner plays Jimmy Wallace, a clean-cut kid who shoots a teenage hoodlum over a girl. Jimmy thinks he killed the hood, so he takes a few hostages and spends the better part of the film's 61 minutes brooding about it. Meanwhile, TV cameras and ghoulish onlookers are attracted like flies. *Cry Baby Killer* is entertaining given its shoestring budget, and Nicholson is compellingly green.[1]

Veteran actor Harry Lauter offers a committed performance as a police lieutenant who tries to patiently negotiate with the volatile Jimmy. Another veteran in the cast is Bill Erwin as Jimmy's father. Erwin is best known for his later appearances on TV's *Seinfeld* during the 1990s. And in the role of Carole Fields is Carolyn Mitchell in her third and final film appearance. Her real name is Barbara Thompson. She would achieve a certain infamy as Mickey Rooney's fifth wife, mother of four of his children. In 1966, at the age of only twenty-nine, she was murdered by a man with whom she was having an affair, with a gun given to her for protection by Rooney. The man then turned the weapon on himself.

While *The Cry Baby Killer* is of little note other than its importance as being Jack Nicholson's theatrical film debut, his next movie, also for Corman, would be far better known. *The Little Shop of Horrors* would have an even lower budget and shorter shooting schedule than *The Cry Baby Killer*, and Nicholson would have a much smaller part. But it would have a much bigger impact on Nicholson's career, on Roger Corman's career, and on its era.

THE LITTLE SHOP OF HORRORS
(1960, Santa Clara Productions/Filmgroup)

★ ★ ★

Director: Roger Corman
Screenplay: Charles B. Griffith
Producer: Roger Corman. *Cinematographer:* Archie Dalzell. *Editor:* Marshall
    Neilan Jr.
Cast: Jonathan Haze (Seymour Krelboyne), Jackie Joseph (Audrey Fulquard),
    Mel Welles (Gravis Mushnick), Dick Miller (Bursou Fouch), Myrtle
    Vail (Winifred Krelboyne), Tammy Windsor (Shirley), Toby Michaels
    (Shirley's friend), Leola Wendorff (Siddie Shiva), Lynn Storey
    (Hortense Fishtwanger), Wally Campo (Sgt. Joe Fink/Narrator),
    Jack Warford (Detective Stoolie), Merri Welles (Leona Clyde), John
    Herman Shaner (Phoebus Farb), Jack Nicholson (Wilbur Force), Dodie
    Drake (Waitress), Charles B. Griffith (several characters)
Released: August 5, 1960
Specs: 72 minutes; black and white
Availability: This film is in the public domain; it is widely available on home
    video

The story of how maverick low-budget filmmaker Roger Corman shot and produced his quickie features has been told so many different ways, one has to piece together the most likely anecdotes in order to come anywhere near accuracy. Corman was a clever cinematic visionary who was able to complete entertaining vehicles in a manner of days using standing sets, borrowing props, and even printing only two or three copies of the script, tearing out pages for actors with speaking parts to share. He often had two cameras filming at once and rarely did retakes. His films were often dismissed as throwaways by the critics. However, the cheap, aggressive nature and tongue-in-cheek humor in his best work has lived on. *The Little Shop of Horrors* is one of the more celebrated cult films of its time, later spawning a Broadway show and a musical movie update in 1986.

The Little Shop of Horrors features a quirky script about Seymour, a timid man nurturing a plant in a flower shop that becomes a talking, carnivorous monster. In order to satisfy his creation, Seymour is forced to kill. In 1960 when this film was released, such a movie as *The Little Shop of Horrors* would appear quite ridiculous to the mainstream. Silly scenes with Seymour pulling body parts out of a bag to feed the plant, with no attempt to hide how phony the props look, would be accepted at face value and not embraced as satirical. To the average moviegoer of the era, *The Little Shop of Horrors* was just a cheap movie with bad effects and aggressive performances. However, to audiences of cult movies that appreciate Corman's vision and screenwriter Griffith's sense of humor, *The Little Shop of Horrors* is a lot of bizarre fun. There is an air of silliness that is continuous throughout. Supper at Seymour's mother's house includes cod liver oil soup, and dinner table conversation includes this exchange:

> *Mom:* Seymour, you promised you wouldn't get married until you bought me an iron lung.
>
> *Seymour:* You've been breathing for years, Ma.
>
> *Mom:* It ain't easy, son.

In a book examining the essential Jack Nicholson films, *The Little Shop of Horrors* has a somewhat different status. Nicholson, still quite new to movies, has a small role. His later stardom resulted in video copies playing up his appearance. Nicholson plays Wilbur Force, a masochist who comes to visit a dentist in order to endure (and enjoy) the pain he is said to provide. However, Seymour has just gotten into a conflict with this dentist and knocked him out. Mistaking Seymour for the doctor, Wilbur insists on being treated. Seymour disposes of the dentist and agrees to treat Wilbur, who states, "No Novocain. It dulls the senses."

Nicholson in *The Little Shop of Horrors. United Artists / Photofest © United Artists*

Nicholson later recalled,

> I went into the shoot knowing I had to be very quirky because Roger originally hadn't wanted me. In other words, I couldn't play it straight. So I just did a lot of weird shit that I thought would make it funny. At a preview, the audience laughed so hard I could barely hear the dialogue. I didn't quite register it right. It was as if I had forgotten it was a comedy since the shoot. I got all embarrassed because I'd never really had such a positive response before.[1]

Nicholson plays the character in a delightfully comic manner. Wilbur is a soft-spoken, meek sort, but his interest in pain is obvious. He sits in the waiting room reading a magazine called *PAIN* and giggles through an article about a man with a hole in his stomach. When the inexperienced Seymour begins working on Wilbur, the masochistic patient shrieks with a combination of pain and maniacal laughter, causing Seymour to back off. "Oh, don't stop now," a euphoric Wilbur insists. When Seymour has finished the job, a satisfied Wilbur promises to recommend him to all of his friends. Nicholson's only scene is just minutes long, but it was one of the highlights of the movie, even when he was unknown. Now that he is a screen icon, Jack Nicholson's scene in *The Little Shop of Horrors* has even greater interest. Nicholson recalled,

We never did shoot the end of the scene. This movie was pre-lit. You'd go in, plug in the lights, roll the camera, and shoot. We did the take outside the office and went inside the office, plugged in, lit and rolled. Jonathan Haze was up on my chest pulling my teeth out. And in the take, he leaned back and hit the rented dental machinery with the back of his leg and it started to tip over. Roger didn't even call cut. He leapt onto the set, grabbed the tilting machine, and said "Next set, that's a wrap."[2]

The Little Shop of Horrors was shot in only two days on standing sets that were about to be torn down, on a budget of $30,000. Interiors were shot with three cameras in single takes. Exteriors were shot by Charles Griffith and Mel Welles over two weekends. They paid a group of children five cents apiece to run out of a subway tunnel and paid winos to appear as extras for ten cents apiece. Corman had initial trouble finding distribution, but the film finally was released as part of a double feature, first with Mario Bava's *Black Sunday* and later with Corman's *The Last Woman on Earth*. Because Corman did not think *The Little Shop of Horrors* was of any financial interest after its first theatrical run, he did not bother to copyright it, resulting in the film's current public domain status.

While critics were often indifferent and dismissive of Corman's films, some reviewers did get the joke. *Variety* stated, "The acting is pleasantly preposterous. Horticulturalists and vegetarians will love it."[3] It is worth noting that *The Little Shop of Horrors* was filmed around the same time as Alfred Hitchcock's *Psycho*. Both films featured a troubled mama's boy who resorts to murder.

After this project, Nicholson spent the next few years alternating between low-budget movies, TV appearances, and stage work. He would enjoy a larger supporting role in a much better Roger Corman production a few years later.

THE RAVEN

(1963, American International)

★ ★ ★

Director: Roger Corman
Screenplay: Richard Matheson, based on the poem by Edgar Allan Poe
Producers: Samuel Z. Arkoff, James H. Nicholson, Roger Corman.
    Cinematographer: Floyd Crosby. *Editor:* Ronald Sinclair
Cast: Vincent Price (Craven), Peter Lorre (Bedlo), Boris Karloff (Scarabus),
    Hazel Court (Lenore), Olive Sturgess (Estelle Craven), Jack Nicholson
    (Rexford Bedlo), Connie Wallace (Maid), William Baskin (Grimes),
    Dick Johnstone (Roderick Craven), Aaron Saxon (Gort), John Dierkes
    (Craven's Corpse)
Released: January 25, 1963
Specs: 86 minutes; Pathécolor
Availability: DVD (MGM)

Roger Corman alternated his low-budget productions from the exploitation of *The Cry Baby Killer* to the quirkiness of *The Little Shop of Horrors* to film adaptions of Edgar Allan Poe's work. *The Raven* is loosely based on Poe's classic poem. In this movie, Dr. Erasmus Craven, a sorcerer, is visited by a raven that turns out to be a wizard named Dr. Bedlo who had been the victim of a spell. Bedlo wants Craven's help seeking revenge against Dr. Scarabus, who was responsible for cursing him. He informs Craven that he saw the spirit of Craven's deceased wife, Lenore, in Scarabus's castle.

Joined by Craven's daughter Estelle and Bedlo's son Rexford, they plan to seek revenge on Scarabus. Once at the castle, Scarabus is discovered to have joined forces with Lenore's spirit to conduct evil.

It has been said that Roger Corman played everything quite seriously and that his collaborators saw the campiness in the material and offered the proper balance. *The Raven*, however, is played strictly for laughs. The story itself has an underlying seriousness, and the art direction offers a macabre appearance, but it is filled with sarcastic one-liners, occasional slapstick, and comically inspired performances. Vincent Price, Boris Karloff, and Peter Lorre all had experience playing in tongue-in-cheek versions of their horror movie personae. Karloff had appeared in Abbott and Costello movies, Lorre and Karloff were together in the horror comedy *The Boogie Man Will Get You* (1942), and Lorre also did a delightful comic turn in Frank Capra's *Arsenic and Old Lace* (1944). Price's past films had established him in a variety of genres that included comedy before he settled into concentrating on horror.

In a book studying Jack Nicholson's films, we must look most closely at this actor's contribution to these earlier efforts where he does not have a lead or even a controlling supporting role. In his initial scenes, he takes a back seat to the veteran horror stars who were at the forefront and guaranteed the film's eventual box office success. As the soft-spoken, bumbling son of Lorre's character, Nicholson is often shown reacting to what the leading actors are doing in the scene and remains pretty much on the periphery. However, there is a filial conflict between him and Lorre's character, and the two seem to enjoy playing this up for comedy. One dialogue exchange between them goes like this:

> *Bedlo:* I just wanted Scarabus to think I was dead so I could help if he moved against any of you.
>
> *Rexford:* He already has. I almost killed myself coming from Miss Craven's room she's locked in.
>
> *Bedlo:* What are you doing in a lady's room?
>
> *Rexford:* Father, that is beside the point.
>
> *Bedlo (yelling):* I will decide what's beside the point!

Rexford is none too bright, and Nicholson plays him with a consistently bewildered expression. Lorre punctuates his dialogue in his scenes with Nicholson by calling him "idiot" and hitting him.

Nicholson also plays Rexford as blissfully unaware of any obvious danger. When he climbs out on the castle's ledge to spy on Scarabus, he offers an amusingly deadpan approach to the danger involved. When Estelle warns, "You might be killed," Rexford replies with no expression, "I hope not!" It plays better than it reads and fits neatly into the proceedings.

Corman's direction is artful and effective, while each veteran performer offers his own approach to the material. Price plays his role essentially straight, but he is not above making a silly cross-eyed face when a bump into a wall dazes him. Lorre is effectively over the top. Karloff plays his role with utter seriousness, anchoring the proceedings in much the same way he did in films like *Abbott and Costello Meet Dr. Jekyll and Mr. Hyde* (1954) or *The Comedy of Terrors*, which was released later the same year as *The Raven*. Interestingly enough, Karloff appeared with Bela Lugosi in a 1935 film entitled *The Raven*, which was also based on the Poe poem, but that movie is far different in approach and presentation than this one.

The Raven climaxes with an effects-driven duel to the death between Scarabus and Craven, each of them digging up their skills in the black arts, after Bedlo is once again turned into a raven. The battle between them is shot without dialogue and includes the sort of chintzy special effects that a low-budget movie like this could afford (the entire production was shot for $200,000 in fifteen days). Most of it involves some tricky ideas with flashing lights, crosscutting, and close-ups. Corman's composition of shots during this sequence is especially impressive—effectively tilting the camera, offering medium establishing shots of the actors framed by fire, and overhead long shots to encompass all of the action.

Variety appeared to be amused by the tongue-in-cheek approach to the classic Poe material, stating in its review,

> Roger Corman as producer-director takes this premise and develops it expertly as a horror-comedy. The screenplay is a skillful, imaginative narrative of what comes to pass when there comes a rapping at magician Vincent Price's chamber-door by a raven—who else but Peter Lorre, a fellow magician, transformed by another sorcerer (Boris Karloff). Hazel Court as Price's sexy and conniving spouse, Olive Sturgess, his daughter, and Jack Nicholson, Lorre's son, lend effective support.[1]

The trade magazine *Independent Exhibitor's Film Bulletin* approached the movie in much the same manner, stating in its review,

> When one terror trio (Edgar Allan Poe, producer-director Roger Corman, American-International Pictures) teams up with another (Vincent Price, Peter

Lorre, Boris Karloff), the outcome figures to be an entertaining bleeding of horror and ham. That is exactly what is in store for you in this loose, tongue-in-cheek version of Poe's famous chiller poem. Mugging credits go to Lorre, who, as secret agent for Karloff, steals every scene. Corman's direction is first rate in the first half, then the pace lags during the middle section, but picks up again with the magical duel-to-the-death finale. The sets and special effects are eerie and effective.[2]

The only mention of Nicholson in this review is to refer to him as "the attractive romantic interest."

After his stint in *The Little Shop of Horrors*, Nicholson went right into the film *Studs Lonigan* (1960) and spent 1961 and 1962 doing small parts on television, concluding 1962 with a role in the feature *The Broken Land*. He then appeared in *The Raven*. Because of its veteran star power, *The Raven* would likely still maintain its status as a cult favorite even without it including an early appearance by Jack Nicholson. However, Nicholson continued to absorb a great deal during the earlier part of his film career, learning a lot from these experiences. Even years later, in a documentary on the making of *The Shining*, Nicholson is shown marking his script in a manner he'd learned from Boris Karloff on the set of *The Raven*.

The Raven was completed ahead of schedule with a few days of shooting left to go. Roger Corman still had access to the impressive castle sets, so, being a maverick low-budget filmmaker whose creative mind was constantly active, he decided to hastily shoot scenes with Jack Nicholson and Boris Karloff for another feature film during those remaining days. Corman then gathered some young directors and a few stock players, like Dick Miller and Jonathan Haze, to shoot other scenes from which he could effectively construct a feature film for release that boasted the formidable Karloff name in the cast. The result was *The Terror*.

THE TERROR

(1963, American International)

★ ★ ½

Director: Roger Corman
Screenplay: Leo Gordon, Jack Hill
Producer: Roger Corman. *Cinematographer:* John Nicholaus. *Editor:* Stuart
    O'Brien. *Second unit direction:* Francis Ford Coppola, Jack Hill, Monte
    Hellman, Jack Nicholson
Cast: Boris Karloff (Baron Von Leppe), Jack Nicholson (Andre Duvalier),
    Sandra Knight (Helene), Dick Miller (Stefan), Dorothy Neumann
    (Katrina), Jonathan Haze (Gustaf)
Released: June 17, 1963
Specs: 81 minutes; color
Availability: A public domain film that is widely available on DVD from many
    distributors

The Terror is set in France during the eighteen century. Nicholson plays
Lieutenant Andre Duvalier, who is wandering aimlessly trying to find his
regiment, from which he has been separated. He sees a mysterious woman
as he wanders on the coast and follows her, asking for directions to Coldon,
where he may be able to find his regiment. She walks away and does not
speak. Duvalier continues to see this woman, including looking out the window of a castle inhabited by the elderly Baron Von Leppe. Inside the castle,
Duvalier sees a painting of the mysterious woman. Von Leppe reveals that

it is a painting of his wife, who died twenty years earlier. Duvalier knows he has seen her alive and attempts to uncover this mystery. He confronts the Baron and gets him to admit he murdered his wife after finding her in the arms of another man named Eric, while his servant, Stefan, killed Eric. But Duvalier is not convinced. He eventually gets Stefan to confess that the Baron is an imposter. He is actually Eric, who killed the Baron and took over his identity twenty years earlier.

The Terror has the reputation of being fully shot in a couple days on the standing sets for *The Raven*. While Corman did use the remaining days on his schedule for the completed *Raven* to shoot the castle scenes for *The Terror*, which made up the bulk of the movie, he also had second unit directors spend a total of nine months shooting scenes elsewhere for the film. Thus, *The Terror* has, in fact, the longest production schedule of any of Corman's movies. All of Boris Karloff's scenes were done during the four-day shoot on the set for *The Raven*, and he did it for a deferred salary of $15,000, payable if the film made more than $150,000. Karloff would later recall,

> Corman had the sketchiest outline of a story. I read it and begged him not to do it. He said "That's alright Boris, I know what I'm going to do. I want you for two days on this." I was in every shot, of course. Sometimes I was just walking through and then I would change my jacket and walk back. He nearly killed me on the last day. He had me in a tank of cold water for about two hours. After he got me in the can he suspended operations and went off and directed two or three operations to get the money, I suppose. . . . [The sets] were so magnificent. . . . As they were being pulled down around our ears, Roger was dashing around with me and a camera, two steps ahead of the wreckers. It was very funny.[1]

As late as 2013, Roger Corman recalled for interviewer Tim Robey,

> The whole picture was only made because it rained on a Sunday. We were supposed to be playing tennis. I called Leo Gordon. We worked out a story-line, and Leo wrote just the two days in which I used Jack Nicholson and Boris Karloff, before Boris went back to England. Because of my Union commitments I couldn't shoot the rest of the picture. Coppola shot a few days, and then he got a job at Warner Bros and his career took off. Monte Hellman shot a bit of it, Jack Hill shot a bit of it. And on the final day Jack Nicholson said to me, "Roger, every idiot in town has shot part of this picture, let me shoot a day!" So I said, "Go on, be a director for a day." We cut it all together, and frankly, every director had a different interpretation and the picture didn't make any sense whatsoever. I was shooting another picture, so I wrote a quick

scene and had Jack Nicholson throw his co-star Dick Miller up against a wall. He said, "I've been lied to ever since I've come to this castle. Now tell me what has been going on!" At which point Dick Miller explains what the picture has been about. People actually took it seriously and tried to figure it all out, but it had no plot whatsoever, that picture. That didn't stop it making money.[2]

Nicholson has a rather large part here and was also given the opportunity to direct some of the scenes. Thus, it has some importance to the early part of his film career when he was still learning his craft. As Richard Harlan Smith stated for Turner Classic Movies,

> While the Jack Nicholson of *The Terror* hasn't quite matured or coalesced yet into the magnetic leading man of *Five Easy Pieces* (1970), *The Last Detail* (1973) and *Chinatown* (1974), his signature Nicholson-isms are all present and accounted for, from the Devil-may-care flatness of his delivery to the reptilian gaze that Stanley Kubrick would take to its hellish apotheosis in the actor's return to the horror genre in *The Shining* (1980).[3]

The Terror is by no means a good movie, but it is an interesting one. The fact that an entire feature could be made with an improvised script and the separate visions of several directors is rather impressive. How one responds to the finished film can only be subjective. Some will dismiss it as a cheap, labored mess. Others believe it to be a good example of low-budget film-making, improvising with limited materials, that resulted in a releasable feature film.

The castle scenes directed by Corman offer his usual eye for effective shot composition, alternating between medium shots, long shots, and close-ups, and often shooting from above to contain more action, or more negative space, in the frame. These shots, plus the impressive sets, add a certain depth to the proceedings, while Karloff once again anchors each scene with his powerful presence. Jack Nicholson has a central role in the narrative, and his scenes with Karloff are especially impressive. Despite Nicholson's comparative inexperience, he holds his own against the veteran actor, who is completely committed to his role despite the rushed, thread-bare production. It is part gothic horror, part detective mystery, with none of the tongue-in-cheek humor of *The Raven* or offbeat quirky comedy of *The Little Shop of Horrors*.

There is some interest in the fact that directors like Francis Ford Coppola and Monte Hellman contributed to the direction. Hellman would soon direct some western films that helped expand Nicholson's opportunities, and Coppola would, of course, become the noted director of the *Godfather* films. This would be the only time Coppola would direct Nicholson.

The Terror has garnered a rather lofty cult status due to its connection to Corman, to Coppola, to Nicholson, and to Karloff, each of whom has a strong legion of admirers. But unlike some cult films whose cheap, aggressive methods resulted in a solidly entertaining feature film, *The Terror* is of only rudimentary interest due to those involved in its production, as well as its backstory. Poor, grainy, public domain prints of this movie abounded on VHS and DVD until it was restored for Blu-ray and a nicer looking print became available.

In the early 1990s, actor Dick Miller, who plays Stefan, appeared in some newly shot footage to be used to frame *The Terror*, where the film is shown to be presented in flashback. This was an attempt by Corman to re-copyright the movie from its public domain status. Dick Miller has stated that his payment for this footage was the most money he ever received from Corman.[4] *The Terror* has another bit of cult movie trivia: it is the movie being screened at the drive-in theater in Peter Bogdanovich's directorial debut *Targets*.

Sandra Knight, Nicholson's wife at the time, played the mysterious woman. She was pregnant with their daughter during filming, a fact that was not too carefully hidden in some shots.

A film like *The Terror* is by no means great cinema, but its status as a cult favorite due to who was involved makes it essential to the early career of Jack Nicholson. His development and exploring of film's creative process continued.

THE SHOOTING

(1966, Continental Distributing)

★ ★ ★ ★

Director: Monte Hellman
Screenplay: Adrien Joyce (Carole Eastman)
Producers: Monte Hellman, Jack Nicholson. *Cinematographer:* Gregory Sander.
    Editor: Monte Hellman
Cast: Will Hutchins (Coley), Millie Perkins (Woman), Jack Nicholson (Billy
    Spear), Warren Oates (Willett), Charles Eastman (Bearded Man), Gul
    El Tsosie (Indian), Brand Carroll (Sheriff), B. J. Merholz (Leland Drum),
    Wally Moon (Deputy), William Mackleprang (Cross Tree Townsman),
    James Campbell (Cross Tree Townsman)
Released: June 12, 1968, in France. Shown October 23, 1966, at the San
    Francisco Film Festival. Shown February 24, 1971, in Dallas, Texas
Specs: 82 minutes; color
Availability: DVD (Criterion)

Since appearing in *The Terror*, Jack Nicholson had a small role in the feature *Ensign Pulver* (1964), a tardy flop sequel to *Mister Roberts* (1955) with
none of the principals from the previous film's cast. Nicholson also did two
lesser westerns with Monte Hellman: *Flight to Fury* (1964) and *Back Door
to Hell* (1964). These had been filmed back to back and were financed by
Roger Corman. Those films led to the same collaboration for *The Shooting*

and *Ride in the Whirlwind*, which were also filmed consecutively in the same manner.

The screenplay for *The Shooting*, by Carole Eastman (under the name Adrien Joyce), takes a standard revenge plot as found in many westerns and creates a bleak, rather artistic film. The medium shots are expansive, taking advantage of the location scenery that frames the action. The natural light offers an immediacy to the proceedings. And despite the low budget and threadbare crew, Hellman employs tracking shots that further help the pacing as the narrative progresses. *The Shooting* does not showcase Jack Nicholson as an actor as much as it does Oates, Hutchins, and Perkins, but the fact that he was behind its production and has some input as to its concept and vision makes it an essential entry in his filmography.

Warren Oates plays a rugged character who does not trust his companions. Will Hutchins is the quintessentially amiable dimwit, but his contribution is not for comic relief like a western sidekick. It adds a bit of an edge to the dynamic of the three central figures. Millie Perkins is not a damsel in distress who is dependent on virile male leaders. She is a caustic, disagreeable, defiant brat who has hired the men (for $1,000) to help her get to a town called Kingsley. She has no character name, as she refuses to reveal it to the others. Nicholson's character adds to this dynamic when the woman feels the need for the sort of cold-hearted gunslinger attitude that he projects. He does not trust her, nor does he trust her companions. Monte Hellman told *Film International*,

> The initial reaction to Millie was far from enthusiastic. I think mainly because of her high pitched voice running counter to expectations about a powerful woman. Looking at her in the movie today, I'm amazed at what a complex, consistent and spontaneous performance she created. It's easily on par with any of her more seasoned fellow actors, all of whom never cease to astound me.[1]

Along with the offbeat characters, *The Shooting* challenges a lot of western clichés, not unlike the way Sergio Leone spaghetti westerns redefined and expanded the genre while making a star out of Clint Eastwood. In fact, more horses are killed than people.

Cinematically, there are some challenging elements. Hellman avoids dissolves when he changes scenes (perhaps due to the small budget), and he eliminated the first ten pages of the script, believing backstory was not necessary to the narrative. The dialogue is sparse, the characters are reserved, the shots are expansive, and the underlying music is taut and quiet. *The Shooting* is a character study, resting more on individual psychologies

With Millie Perkins in his first western, *The Shooting*. Photofest

than frantic action. It is one of the most interesting films in Nicholson's early career, and it allowed him to learn more about the cinematic process. The film's conclusion leaves more questions than answers, but in a way that makes it intriguing rather than disappointing. *The Shooting* might have been one of the most interesting, offbeat westerns of its time had it received greater theatrical release in its time and been allowed to make an impact at that time. Marc Eliot called it "an incomprehensible fury of a film, with an indecipherable plot. There were lots of cowboys on horses, lots of funs fired, and lots of people (maybe) dying. It is a fascinating attempt at bending a genre (and a couple of minds)."[2]

The Shooting was produced for $75,000, shot with natural light, took three weeks to film, took a year to get through the editing process, received positive reviews at festivals, and could not secure a US release. It was followed by another western, *Ride in the Whirlwind*, which was another three-week shoot, with essentially the same cast and crew. The second film also enjoyed positive reactions at festivals and also could not secure a US release. The distribution rights for both films were sold to a French distributor who went bankrupt, keeping the films tied up in Paris for nearly two years. They were eventually sold to television in 1968, receiving little broadcast. In 1971 a small-time company picked up the distribution rights for both films due to Jack Nicholson's rising fame.

Both movies were shot in 1965, back to back, with six weeks of steady shooting. Roger Corman put up the money for the budget with the understanding that if the movie went over budget, it would be up to producers Monte Hellman and Jack Nicholson to finance any extra costs. Despite all of these various hindrances, both *The Shooting* and *Ride in the Whirlwind* are good westerns, with a nice composition of shots to enhance the narrative and good acting from talented professionals (Nicholson and Hellman basically hired friends to play the roles—but their friends were good actors).

Nicholson recalled for *Film Comment*,

> Roger Corman only financed them because we cheated him, in a way. We told him that one of them was a kind of western African Queen and the other a variation on Fort Apache. But, what we delivered him were two very austere New Wave westerns, and he knew it. Fortunately, the budgets were such that he knew he couldn't lose more than he'd already paid for the scripts. You had to be a little bit of a pirate in those days.[3]

In some studies it is claimed that a week's rest was taken before beginning on *Ride in the Whirlwind*, while most sources indicate the films were shot consecutively over six weeks. In any case, *Ride in the Whirlwind* uses many of the same concepts as *The Shooting* but with decidedly less aesthetic success.

RIDE IN THE WHIRLWIND

(1966, Continental Distributing)

★ ★ ★ ½

Director: Monte Hellman
Screenplay: Jack Nicholson
Producers: Monte Hellman, Jack Nicholson, Roger Corman. *Cinematographer:*
    Gregory Sandor. *Editor:* Monte Hellman
Cast: Jack Nicholson (Wes), Cameron Mitchell (Vern), George Mitchell
    (Evan), Millie Perkins (Abigail), Katherine Squire (Catherine), Rupert
    Crosse (Indian Joe), Harry Dean Stanton (Blind Dick), John Hackett
    (Winslow), Tom Filer (Otis), B. J. Merholz (Edgar), Brandon Carroll
    (Quint Mapes), Peter Cannon (Hagerman), William A. Keller (Roy)
Released: September 11, 1968, in France. Shown October 23, 1966, at the
    San Francisco Film Festival
Specs: 82 minutes; Eastmancolor
Availability: DVD (Criterion)

As discussed in our chapter on *The Shooting, Ride in the Whirlwind* was shot in three weeks after the three-week production of the previous film, and by the same people. And although *The Shooting* is arguably the better film, *Ride in the Whirlwind* might be somewhat more significant in our study of Jack Nicholson's screen work. Along with having a bigger role than the previous movie, Nicholson also wrote the screenplay for this one along with once again co-producing with Hellman and Roger Corman.

Ride in the Whirlwind is about three cowboys who stop to rest in a remote area and wake up to discover they are surrounded by vigilantes who believe them to be three wanted outlaws and plan to hang them. One of the cowboys is killed, but the other two escape to a farm, holding the family hostage. They steal two horses from the farmers amid a shootout where the farm patriarch is killed and one of the fugitives is wounded. The posse continues to pursue the two men as outlaws, despite their innocence, and one of them realizes his wounds are too serious for him to continue. He sacrifices himself to the posse, allowing the other to get away.

There are similarities between Ride in the Whirlwind and The Shooting due to the same production team working on both films. Most notably is Hellman's penchant for using little exposition and little dialogue, allowing visuals to tell the story. His shot composition is once again quite brilliant, as he artfully utilizes expansive long shots and medium shots in order to allow the carefully chosen location scenery to frame the action. Monte Hellman told Film International,

> Ride in the Whirlwind was inspired by a book called Bandits of the Plains which Nicholson came across while researching the screenplay. It consisted of diaries from the period, one of which described a three-day siege similar to the one in our movie.[1]

With a larger role that exhibited the same sort of hesitant delivery and bewildered cynicism he'd displayed in The Shooting, Nicholson is once again very impressive. As stated in the previous chapter, these films were not picked up by a US distributor, not being shown in America until their television release (in the case of Ride in the Whirlwind, that would be in 1968, three years after it had been shot). It is difficult to deal accurately with "what if" predictions, but when we judge Nicholson's work as an actor, it is evident that his performance in The Shooting and Ride in the Whirlwind may very well have ignited his rise to stardom had they been seen by more people at the time each film was produced. He may not have had to wait for Easy Rider a few years later before the mainstream started to take notice.

Casting was once again done carefully and effectively. Cameron Mitchell had been in movies for twenty years; Harry Dean Stanton for ten. Millie Perkins had been a child actress, making an immediate impact in her film debut as the title character in The Diary of Anne Frank. Perkins had offered a strong performance in The Shooting and was used again for this film. She had been friendly with both Nicholson and Hellman since all three were taking acting lessons years earlier. Monte Hellman told Film International,

Almost any movie will become a completely different animal depending on casting. I am fascinated by people. I fall in love with the people I'm working with, and once the process begins, I find these people much more interesting than any characters on the pages of the script. During the course of my creative life I became increasingly aware of this bent and found ways to encourage my actors to allow the character to become them, rather than the other way around.[2]

Although most prefer *The Shooting* among the two films, biographer Patrick McGilligan stated in his book *Jack's Life*,

> *The Shooting* became the more acclaimed of the Westerns, and over time has gained a cult status in France as well as elsewhere. But [*Ride in the Whirlwind*] was excellent in its own right and a few critics thought it the more accessible and enjoyable of the shoestring shoot-em-ups.[3]

And while Peter Sobczynski prefers *The Shooting* in his DVD review of the two films, his 2014 assessment gives us some understanding of how the movies both grew in status and are basically as good as each other:

> If pressed to demonstrate a preference for one over the other, I suppose that I would finally have to side with *The Shooting* though that is less the result of any real deficiencies in *Ride in the Whirlwind* and more because *The Shooting* offers up the sight of the great Warren Oates [who would work several times with Hellman over the years] in one of his first lead roles. Nevertheless, both are astonishing films that play beautifully today and deserve to be considered among the great latter-day westerns.[4]

The lack of distribution for *The Shooting* and *Ride in the Whirlwind* kept Jack Nicholson's brilliant performance in either film from igniting his career with the mainstream. His next film was a dismissive biker movie entitled *Hells Angels on Wheels* (1967), which only generated some marginal interest because his breakthrough was another, more famous biker movie, *Easy Rider*, a couple of years later. He also had a small, uncredited role in Roger Corman's *The St. Valentine's Day Massacre* (1967), and did some stints on such TV shows as *The Guns of Will Sonnett* and *The Andy Griffith Show*.

Jack Nicholson then appeared in Richard Rush's *Psych Out* (1968), for which he submitted the script. Rush found Nicholson's vision too edgy for the mainstream, so E. Hunter Willett, Betty Ulius, and Betty Tusher reworked it, with Nicholson receiving no writing credit. He still acts in the film as a character he'd created, but the movie about flower power and the drug culture of Haight-Ashbury has dated badly, even as a cultural throw-back. Nicholson's next essential effort had him team with Bob Rafelson for a film that maintained all of its edginess, its surrealism, its experimental approach, and its psychedelic presentation, with its only mainstream element being that it was about the TV-generated pop music group the Monkees.

HEAD

(1968, Columbia)

★ ★ ½

Director: Bob Rafelson
Screenplay: Bob Rafelson, Jack Nicholson
Producers: Bob Rafelson, Jack Nicholson. *Cinematographer:* Michel Hugo.
    Editors: Mike Pozen, Monte Hellman
Cast: The Monkees (Micky Dolenz, Davy Jones, Mike Nesmith, Peter Tork),
    Victor Mature (The Big Victor), Annette Funicello (Minnie), Timothy
    Carey (Lord High 'n Low), Logan Ramsey (Officer Faye Lapid),
    Abraham Sofaer (Swami), Charles Maccaulay (Inspector Shrink), T. C.
    Jones (Mr. and Mrs. Ace), Charles Irving (Mayor Feedback), William
    Bagdad (Haraldic Messenger), Carol Doda (Sally Silicone), Frank Zappa
    (The Critic), June Fairchild (The Jumper), Teri Garr (Testy True),
    Mireille Machu (Lady Pleasure), Terry Chambers (hero), Mike Burns
    (Nothing), Esther Shepard (Mother), Jim Hanley (Frodis). Cameos
    by Vito Scotti, Ray Nitschke, Sonny Liston, Rona Barrett, Toni Basil,
    Dennis Hopper, Tor Johnson, Tiger Joe Marsh, Jack Nicholson, Jo
    Anne Worley, Bob Rafelson
Songs: "Porpoise Song" (performed by the Monkees; composed by Gerry
    Goffin and Carole King); "Ditty Diego" (performed by the Monkees;
    composed by Jack Nicholson and Bob Rafelson); "Circle Sky"
    (performed by the Monkees; composed by Michael Nesmith); "Can
    You Dig It" (performed by the Monkees; composed by Peter Tork);
    "As We Go Along" (performed by the Monkees; composed by Carole
    King and Toni Stern); "Daddy's Song" (performed by the Monkees;
    composed by Harry Nilsson [as Nilsson])

> *Released:* November 20, 1968
> *Specs:* 86 minutes (director's cut 110 minutes); Technicolor and black and
>   white
> *Availability:* DVD (Rhino)

The enormous popularity of the Beatles inspired producers Bob Rafelson and Bert Schneider to create a TV show based on the quirky comedy of the group's movie *A Hard Day's Night* (1964) and repackage it for the mainstream teen audience. Hiring two actors who could sing and two musicians who could sing and act, Rafelson and Schneider created *The Monkees*. They asked Don Kirshner, who was the Screen Gems head of music, to find songs for the Monkees to record. Kirshner hired songwriters Tommy Boyce and Bobby Hart, who composed the TV show's theme song and also the group's first big hit, "Last Train to Clarksville." The Monkees' tunes would also draw from the songwriting talents of Neil Diamond ("I'm a Believer" and "A Little Bit Me, a Little Bit You"), Carole King ("Pleasant Valley Sunday"), and John Stewart ("Daydream Believer"), while the group would even pen some tracks themselves. The TV show premiered in 1966 and was a huge hit, as were the carefully crafted and shrewdly marketed pop songs that were released to Top 40 radio.

By 1968, the Monkees' career had dwindled. Their fans got older, more sophisticated, and gravitated toward the likes of Jimi Hendrix, who'd once been their opening act. In an attempt to reinvent their image, the group agreed to appear in an offbeat piece of experimental cinema concocted by Rafelson and Jack Nicholson, in which the Monkees would confront their manufactured image. Rather than reinvent them, *Head* destroyed what little the Monkees had left, and the group soon disbanded. Their TV show continued in reruns, however; there were a few reunions over the years, and the charm of their pop songs continued to be fondly remembered into the twenty-first century.

Head is a fascinating look at how show business devours its own. Nicholson's rewrite of the group's theme song opens the film:

Hey, hey, we are the Monkees
You know we love to please
A manufactured image
With no philosophies.
You say we're manufactured.

To that we all agree.
So make your choice and we'll rejoice
in never being free!
Hey, hey, we are the Monkees
We've said it all before
The money's in, we're made of tin
We're here to give you more!

From this point the film is a messy pastiche of unrelated vignettes that challenge not only the Monkees' harmless pop image, but also the cinematic process and any linear narrative structure. Sequences in outer space, in a western setting, during a military war, in a desert, and so on, are all presented, but conclude quickly without wrapping anything up. Footage of screaming fans at a concert is interspersed with explosions on a battlefield. The boys are shot at in a foxhole, do elaborate death scenes, and then get up and continue with the next piece of dialogue. Micky is shown addressing the director and saying, "I quit, Bob." Peter balks when a scene calls for him to hit a woman, believing it will destroy his image with his young fans.

The film doesn't hold together at all. But at the same time, there are enough bizarre, clever ideas to make it interesting. The Monkees were natural performers and had, by now, become quite comfortable in the roles they'd been playing for years on their weekly TV series. Some of the music is quite good in the Monkees tradition, but none of the songs emerged as hits. But, most of all, the film was an enormous financial failure. While some of its aesthetic qualities are notable and it has since achieved a certain cult appreciation, the world of mainstream cinema was not ready for *Head*, nor were the Monkees' remaining fans. The critics were especially caustic. *Variety* stated,

> *Head* is an extension of the ridiculous nonsense served up on the Screen Gems vidseries that manufactured The Monkees and lasted two full seasons following the same format and, ostensibly, appealing to the same kind of audience.[1]

While Vincent Canby of the *New York Times* tried to make something out of the film, he was ultimately confused:

> There are some funny moments—an old joke about a regiment of Italian soldiers surrendering to a single man, a policeman posing girlishly before a mirror, a scene in which the boys are cast as dandruff in the hair of a giant Victor Mature, a war scene in which Ray Nitschke of the Green Bay Packers keeps senselessly tackling a G. I., an attack on a Coke machine, a breaking up

of the film set, a nice transposition of the Columbia Pictures logo. There are some ugly scenes, too—mock fights in which Sonny Liston badly beats one of the Monkees about the face.[2]

In a 2012 interview with *Rolling Stone*, Mike Nesmith stated,

By the time *Head* came out the Monkees were a pariah. There was no confusion about this. We were on the cosine of the line of approbation, from acceptance to rejection . . . and it was basically over. *Head* was a swan song. We wrote it with Jack and Bob . . . and we liked it. It was an authentic representation of a phenomenon we were a part of that was winding down. It was very far from suicide—even though it may have looked like that. There were some people in power, and not a few critics, who thought there was another decision that could have been made. But I believe the movie was an inevitability—there was no other movie to be made that would not have been ghastly under the circumstances.[3]

At this point in his career, Jack Nicholson was taking various acting jobs in low-budget films that sometimes did not see release and TV shows where he could count on steady income, while also investigating other areas of filmmaking as a writer, producer, and sometime co-director. After he achieved some level of stardom, he would continue to look back fondly at *Head* as a surreal response to the manufactured fame of a pop group that was created in a board room, but still enjoyed a hit TV series and several huge hit songs and albums. The fact that the Monkees' music has lived on over decades and with new generations makes this concept more interesting today than it was in 1968.

Jack Nicholson could not possibly have realized that he was on the cusp of stardom at this time. When he was asked to play a supporting role in a film being done by his friends Peter Fonda and Dennis Hopper, he accepted the part. It might have been as successful as one of his Roger Corman movies; it might get buried like his Monte Hellman westerns. Bob Rafelson would join Fonda as one of the producers, and the film would be made in association with his and Bert Schneider's Raybert productions. So, after the debacle of *Head*, Jack Nicholson went to work on the film *Easy Rider*.

EASY RIDER

(1969, Columbia)

★ ★ ★ ½

Director: Dennis Hopper
Screenplay: Peter Fonda, Dennis Hopper, Terry Southern
Producer: Peter Fonda. *Cinematographer:* Laszlo Kovacs. *Editors:* Donn
    Cambern, Henry Jaglom, Marilyn Schlossberg, Stan Siegel, Bruce
    Conner
Cast: Peter Fonda (Wyatt); Dennis Hopper (Billy); Phil Spector (Connection);
    Mac Mashourian (Bodyguard); Warren Finnerty (Rancher); Tita
    Colorado (Rancher's Wife); George Jack Nicholson (George Hanson);
    Karen Black (Karen); Luke Askew (Stranger on Highway); Luana
    Anders (Lisa); Sabrian Scharf (Sarah); Sandy Wyeth (Joanne); Robert
    Walker Jr. (Jack); George Fowler Jr. (Guard); Keith Green (Sheriff);
    Toni Basil (Mary); Lea Marmer (Madame); David Billodeau, Johnny
    David (Pickup Truck Shooters); Bridget Fonda, Justin Fonda (Children
    in Commune); Dan Haggerty (Man in Commune); Carrie Snodgrass,
    Helena Kallianiotes (Women in Commune)
Songs: "The Pusher" (performed by Steppenwolf; composed by Hoyt
    Axton); "Born to Be Wild" (performed by Steppenwolf; composed
    by Mars Bonfire); "I Wasn't Born to Follow" (performed by the
    Byrds; composed by Gerry Goffin and Carole King); "The Weight"
    (performed by the Band; composed by Robbie Robertson [as Jaime
    Robbie Robertson]); "If You Want to Be a Bird" (performed by
    the Holy Modal Rounders; composed by Antonia Duren); "Don't
    Bogart Me" (performed by Fraternity of Man; composed by Elliot

Ingber and Larry Wagner); "If Six Was Nine" (performed by the Jimi Hendrix Experience; composed by Jimi Hendrix); "Let's Turkey Trot" (performed by Little Eva; composed by Gerry Goffin and Jack Keller); "Kyrie Eleison" (performed by the Electric Prunes; composed by David A. Axelrod); "Flash, Bam, Pow" (performed by Electric Flag; composed by Mike Bloomfield); "It's Alright Ma (I'm Only Bleeding)" (performed by Roger McGuinn; composed by Bob Dylan); "Ballad of Easy Rider" (performed by Roger McGuinn; composed by Roger McGuinn)
Released: June 26, 1969
Specs: 95 minutes; color and black and white
Availability: DVD (Columbia/Sony)

Easy Rider is noteworthy as the film that made Jack Nicholson a star. From this point, he would secure stronger billing and his stardom would rise with each successive movie until superstardom and, eventually, iconic status would be earned. Nicholson has a supporting role in *Easy Rider*, appearing only in the last half of the movie, but his performance stands out and resonates. His character is also the most interesting one in the film.

Nicholson had already collaborated with Peter Fonda and Dennis Hopper on the film *The Trip* (1967), and had acted in the biker movies *Hells Angels on Wheels* (1967) and *The Rebel Rousers* (1970), which had been filmed around the same time as *Hells Angels on Wheels* but not released until a few years later. Peter Fonda had appeared in *The Wild Angels* (1966) and from that experience got the idea to do a modern-day western with motorcyclists as cowboys; hence the central characters being named Billy (for Billy the Kid) and Wyatt (for Wyatt Earp).

American cinema had entered the counterculture with the box office success of films like *Bonnie and Clyde* and *The Graduate* (both 1967). Peter Fonda was a part of the cinematic counterculture, not only due to *The Wild Angels*, but also because of *The Trip*, which he produced from Nicholson's screenplay. As an independent filmmaker, Fonda's success, and perhaps his lineage, allowed for some funding so that he could produce *Easy Rider* from his vision. Fonda secured Dennis Hopper as director and collaborated on the screenplay with both Hopper and Terry Southern. Hopper mostly hired friends for the cast and crew, while both Fonda and Southern also made such contributions. Originally, Rip Torn, a friend of Southern's, was set to play the character of George Hanson, but a conflict with Hopper resulted in Nicholson being hired for the role. Apparently, Hopper was speaking negatively about "rednecks" in the southern states. Rip Torn, a

Texan, took offense, and the two almost came to blows. Nicholson and Hopper had no such issues.

The story of *Easy Rider* opens by introducing Wyatt (whose nickname is Captain America) and Billy as they smuggle cocaine from Mexico to Los Angeles and sell it to their United States connection. They then decide to head to New Orleans for Mardi Gras. On the way they meet an assortment of different characters, from ranchers to hippies, spending some time in a commune that struggles with gardening in the hot sun and little rain. They sing songs, put on plays, and function within their own egalitarian society that wavers between interesting and unsettling to Billy and Wyatt.

These earlier scenes start the film out very slowly, showing us that there is no real plot structure. The location scenery is beautiful, and Hopper, as director, offers wide shots to show the bikers as small moving figures in the foreground, surrounded by mountain ranges and other majestic beauty. The soundtrack enhances the peace and tranquility of this absolute freedom, not unlike a conventional western. However, these are bikers and the musical background contains rock-oriented songs by Steppenwolf, the Byrds, and the Band. That some of the music displays rock's country influence makes its connection to a western-oriented theme more discernible.

Jack Nicholson appears when Wyatt and Billy are arrested for disrupting a parade and put in jail. It is there that they meet American Civil Liberties Union lawyer George Hanson, a drunk who has been jailed for repeated offenses. They are attracted to his carefree, philosophical manner. When all three are freed the next day, George joins Wyatt and Billy on their trek to New Orleans. When the three camp for the night, George is introduced to marijuana.

It is perhaps this scene that most effectively secured Nicholson the Oscar nomination he would eventually get for this performance. While George is a savvy lawyer, his backwoods background exhibits a real naïveté when Captain America offers him a joint. "I have enough trouble with the booze and all, I don't want to get hooked," he says, adding, "It leads to harder stuff." Along with applying a harsher level of danger to marijuana, he smokes it incorrectly when finally convinced it is not as harmful as he believes. He inhales and exhales as one would a standard tobacco cigarette and has to be coached by Captain American to hold the smoke in longer. As George tokes, he becomes more talkative, explaining UFOs and aliens "from within our own solar system, except their society is more highly evolved," saying that they have no war and that they live "equally and with no effort." It is the fantasy that all three men have for America, despite Wyatt dismissing it as a "crackpot idea." It is not the concept; it is the idea of there being aliens

With Peter Fonda in *Easy Rider,* which earned Nicholson his first Oscar nomination. *Columbia Pictures; photographer: Peter Sorel / Photofest © Columbia Pictures*

in space. When Wyatt asks why the spacemen to which George refers do not reveal themselves, George responds matter-of-factly, stating that such a revelation would cause a general panic.

Throughout the entire scene, Nicholson is firmly in the spotlight as George is the center of attention. Both Wyatt and Billy focus on him and what he is saying. Alternating between seriousness and smiling whimsy, Nicholson presents George as more of a dreamer than a crackpot, despite the rather outrageous things he is saying.

During a stop to eat at a small-town Louisiana restaurant, the three men are mocked by local redneck stereotypes for the way they look. Hopper films the scene expertly, editing between close-ups of the rednecks making a running commentary as to how the three men are "queers" and "animals" who aren't even good enough to be placed in their jail because "jail is for humanity" and the three men who quietly, stoically listen without responding, other than George referring to what they are saying as "country witticisms." The three leave the restaurant without being served. Later that night as they are camping, George states, "This used to be a hell of a good country. I can't understand what's gone wrong with it." It results in this dialogue between George and Wyatt:

> *Wyatt:* They're scared of us.
>
> *George:* They're not scared of you. They're scared of what you represent. What you represent to them is freedom.
>
> *Wyatt:* What the hell is wrong with freedom? That's what it's all about.
>
> *George:* Oh yeah that's what it's all about all right. But talking about it and being it, that's two different things. Don't ever tell anybody that they ain't free because they'll kill and maim to prove they are.

During the night they are tracked down by the rednecks and beaten. Wyatt and Billy get up to fight back and end up not being hurt too badly. However, George is killed, thus ending Nicholson's appearance in the film.

From this point Wyatt and Billy end up in a New Orleans brothel that George had recommended, pick up two prostitutes, spend the night in a cemetery, and then venture to Florida, where the men plan to retire with their money from drug deals. They are spotted on the road by two more rednecks in a pickup, who aim a gun at them in an attempt to frighten them. Wyatt responds by flipping them off, and both men are shot dead on the road.

Upon completing filming of *Easy Rider* during the spring of 1968, Hopper ended up with a rough cut that exceeded four hours. Many editors worked on it, including filmmaker Henry Jaglom, who came up with the ninety-five-minute edit that was eventually released. Initially, Hopper was unhappy with the result, complaining his film was turned into a TV movie. But once the movie was released and enjoyed good reviews and strong box office, he changed his mind.

Although *Easy Rider* extended from the cinematic counterculture subgenre that included *The Graduate* and *Bonnie and Clyde*, today it does not hold up as well as those other films. Much of the attitude appears dated, and hardly presents itself as progressive or open-minded as it might have seemed to younger people as far back as 1969. The psychedelic sequence in the cemetery, as Hopper experiments with editing techniques and off-kilter visuals, might have seemed arty at the time but comes off as distracting and confusing in the twenty-first century. The quick cuts and alternating lights and colors interspersed with religious imagery don't serve much aesthetic purpose.

The one thing that does continue to stand out in *Easy Rider* is Jack Nicholson's star-making performance. It uses elements of character that can be traced all the way back to *The Cry Baby Killer*, his film debut, and although he has a small part, Nicholson's standout performance displays how he has honed the elements of the various roles he'd played up to that point. And while he did not win the Oscar for Best Supporting Actor, his nomination signaled that he had indeed arrived and was now a star in his own right. Nicholson did win a Golden Laurel award and a New York Critics award for his performance.

Easy Rider was the fourth most profitable film of 1969, behind *Butch Cassidy and the Sundance Kid*, *The Love Bug*, and *Midnight Cowboy*, which shows how diverse American mainstream cinema had been that year. It took in $60 million worldwide and $47 million domestically. In 1998 it was added to the United States National Film Registry, having been deemed "culturally, historically, or aesthetically significant." And it made Jack Nicholson a star. The success of this film also resulted in Dennis Hopper receiving funding and creative control to make another movie, but *The Last Movie* (1971) flopped and turned out to have a rather prophetic title.

In Jack Nicholson's subsequent film, he had the lead role, just as he'd had in *The Cry Baby Killer*, his movie debut. Only this time, Jack Nicholson also had a name that was expected to draw in the moviegoers.

FIVE EASY PIECES

(1970, Columbia)

★ ★ ★ ★ ★

Director: Bob Rafelson
Screenplay: Carole Eastman (as Adrien Joyce). *Story:* Bob Rafelson
Producers: Bob Rafelson, Richard Wechsler. *Cinematographer:* László Kovács.
    Editors: Christopher Holmes, Gerald Shepard
Cast: Jack Nicholson (Robert Eroica Dupea), Karen Black (Rayette Dipesto),
    Billy Green Bush (Elton), Fannie Flagg (Stoney), Sally Struthers (Betty),
    Marlena MacGuire (Twinky), Richard Stahl (Recording Engineer), Lois
    Smith (Partita), Helena Kallianiotes (Palm Apodaca), Toni Basil (Terry
    Grouse), Lorna Thayer (Waitress), Susan Ansphach (Catherine Von
    Oost), Ralph Waite (Carl), William Challee (Nicholas), John Ryan
    (Spicer), Clay Greenbush (Baby)
Released: September 12, 1970
Specs: 98 minutes; color
Availability: DVD (Criterion)

In one of the strongest performances of his entire career, Jack Nicholson elevated *Five Easy Pieces* to classic status, especially due to a couple of standout scenes. One represents the implosion of 1960s counterculture attitudes as the 1970s begin. The other allows Nicholson to dig very deeply and exhibit a level of unbridled emotion, the likes of which he'd thereafter continue to revisit on occasion.

Nicholson plays Bobby, a trained classical pianist from a high-level artistic family who has estranged himself from his father and embraced a lifestyle that is far removed from his upbringing. Bobby prefers the life of a California oil field worker who bowls, drinks, cheats on his waitress girlfriend, and never settles down. It is the life he has chosen, and he's comfortable within its limitations because of his irresponsible freedoms. When Bobby's life becomes complicated—girlfriend Rayette is pregnant and best friend Elton has been put in jail—he decides to remove himself from his current situation. He quits his job and heads to Los Angeles to visit his sister, also a pianist, who is currently recording an album. When Bobby arrives, he is informed that his father has suffered several strokes and hasn't long to live. Bobby's sister convinces him to go to Washington State and say goodbye as closure.

Within the first half hour of the movie, the narrative presents many layers to Bobby's character. He is alternately focused and distracted, satisfied and restless. He appears to have settled completely into his working-class life, but when he sees a piano on the back of a moving junk truck, he hops

Nicholson received his second Oscar nomination—and first for a leading role—in *Five Easy Pieces. Columbia Pictures / Photofest © Columbia Pictures*

on the truck and starts playing Chopin, completely oblivious to where the vehicle is headed. He seems to connect comfortably with his friends, but when Elton reveals to him that Rayette is pregnant, he not only balks at the impending responsibility, but also haughtily chastises Elton for being a "redneck"—"How dare you compare your life to mine?"—showing some connection to his breeding despite his having left it behind. In Los Angeles, with his sister, his persona changes. Bobby is now clad in a jacket and tie instead of working-class denim. His hair is neatly combed. He seems as removed from his oil-rigging world as he seemed separated from his artistic life while living among the working class.

However, the connection to Rayette isn't going to sever easily. When Bobby packs to go see his father in Washington, Rayette threatens to commit suicide if he leaves her. Bobby is filled with tension at the prospect of seeing his father, from who he'd been estranged, and now has the added stress of Rayette's threatening ultimatum. This pent-up anger manifests itself in the car as he yells and flails his arms before going back into the house and reluctantly asking Rayette to accompany him.

Bobby's world has gone from the simple life of a working man, far estranged from the life from which he had fled, to a series of complex difficulties. These problems exist in both of his worlds, and now they threaten to clash as Rayette accompanies him in his journey back home. This leads to one of the film's most iconic scenes.

As they venture toward Washington, Bobby and Rayette find two women on the side of the road whose car has been wrecked. They are headed to Alaska. Bobby agrees to give them a ride as far as Washington. This sets up the dynamic between the four people, who become friendly and manage to connect as the car moves along. The film's counterculture theme is explored via one of the girls, who sits in the back seat and emotionally discusses the capitalist society and a nation that amounts to "so much crap" and "so much filth." The dialogue in the car sets up the scene where the four of them stop at a diner, and Bobby has this exchange with the waitress:

Bobby: I'd like a plain omelet, no potatoes, tomatoes instead, a cup of coffee, and wheat toast.

Waitress: No substitutions.

Bobby: What do you mean? You don't have any tomatoes?

Waitress: Only what's on the menu. You can have a number two—a plain omelet. It comes with cottage fries and rolls.

Bobby: Yeah, I know what it comes with, but it's not what I want.

Waitress: Well, I'll come back when you make up your mind.

Bobby: Wait a minute. I have made up my mind. I'd like a plain omelet, no potatoes on the plate, a cup of coffee, and a side order of wheat toast.

Waitress: I'm sorry. We don't have any side orders of toast. I'll give you an English muffin or a coffee roll.

Bobby: What do you mean you don't make side orders of toast? You make sandwiches, don't you?

Waitress: Would you like to talk to the manager?

Bobby: You've got bread and a toaster of some kind?

Waitress: I don't make the rules.

Bobby: Okay, I'll make it as easy for you as I can. I'd like an omelet, plain, and a chicken salad sandwich on wheat toast, no mayonnaise, no butter, no lettuce, and a cup of coffee.

Waitress: A number two, chicken salad sandwich, hold the butter, the lettuce, and the mayonnaise, and a cup of coffee. Anything else?

Bobby: Yeah. Now all you have to do is hold the chicken, bring me the toast, give me a check for the chicken salad sandwich, and you haven't broken any rules.

Waitress: You want me to hold the chicken, huh?

Bobby: I want you to hold it between your knees.

The waitress then asks the group to leave, whereupon Bobby pushes the water glasses off the table onto the floor with a big, sweeping gesture of his arm. Back in the car, one of the girls congratulates his audacity, whereupon Bobby responds, "I didn't get what I wanted, did I?" He realizes that he ultimately lost the battle.

While this scene only runs a few minutes, it not only stands out as a highlight of the movie, it has become an iconic piece of cinema. Bobby's order is limited by the structured rules of the restaurant. He tries to cleverly defy those rules. Despite this cleverness, his reaction is insulting enough to get them all thrown out. His violent response is impulsive but ultimately futile. He did not get the order he wanted. He got no food at all. Nicholson beautifully exhibits Bobby's pent-up rage. Remaining tense because he is traveling to see his estranged father, a tension further increased by Rayette's situation, Bobby snaps at the restaurant's structured set of rules after a futile attempt to be measured and in control. It is a beautifully played scene and continues to be one of the most representative moments in Jack Nicholson's film career. Bobby's tension, his idiosyncratic behavior, his rebellious spirit, and his attempt to work through the structured rules that limit his freedom are all examined in the restaurant scene. It is an exceptional piece of film despite having little to do with the narrative. It provides comic relief while also offering a bit of social commentary.

Arriving at his father's place, Bobby is reunited with his brother, Carl, and once again sees his sister. His father is catatonic and unaware of who Bobby is. Still, Bobby stays, reconnecting with his family in a series of scenes that show why he likely left the family and stayed away for three years. His exuberance and easy humor are considered boorish by his pretentious siblings, while it is revealed that his father had been cold and judgmental. Adding to this uncomfortable situation, Bobby has to maintain contact, by phone, with Rayette, who is staying elsewhere while he deals with family matters. Finally, he must also work through his attraction to his brother's protégé, Catherine, a pretty young musician.

Bobby's character continues to be a series of contradictions. He voluntary left the life of a musician, but weeps when he plays a piece in his family home because, as he says, "I played it better when I was eight years old." He left this world and is now saddened that he can no longer simply reconnect with the talent he'd once exhibited. While Bobby is playing, director Rafelson chooses to have the camera pan over pictures of Bobby's family and the life he could have had.

Bobby resettles into the comfort of the posh family home, but also reacts angrily to his brother's protégé, pointing out her bath oils and perfumes, asking, "What are you doing with all this crap?" He seems to like and respect his brother, but still has sex with the protégé. Bobby had separated from his father, but now is emotionally stirred by the fact that his father's current condition does not allow him to reconnect at any level. He has lost his last chance to bond. The scene in which Bobby wheels his father out into a secluded area and tries to communicate is another example of Nicholson's best work. Bobby sits in front of his father, whose blank stare indicates he is unable to absorb any of the conversation, and says, "I move around a lot. Not because I'm looking for anything in particular. I just have to get away from things once they get bad." Eventually Bobby descends into sobs. "The best that I can do is apologize." Nicholson is said to have written some of the dialogue he uses in this scene.

Once Bobby leaves the family home behind and goes off with Rayette, he becomes especially introspective, angrily rebuffing Rayette's flirty advances in the car as he ponders the enormity of what he has just experienced.

When they stop at a gas station, Bobby gives Rayette his wallet and she goes in to get coffee. Bobby goes into the men's room and continues to ponder his situation. As he exits the restroom, he tells a trucker that his car has been destroyed in an accident and he needs a lift. Bobby hops onto the truck, which pulls out of the station and heads north. Rayette is stranded, but she has the car and all of Bobby's money. Once again, Bobby has run away from "things once they get bad."

Five Easy Pieces perfectly portrays the concept of alienation. Bobby doesn't want to live his current life; he obviously looks down on his redneck friends, but he doesn't fit into his family's way of life either. A good portion of his personality has to do with him being a creative person; he continuously acts impulsively, but then regrets that he did and that he can't do anything better with himself. *Five Easy Pieces* further shows Jack Nicholson's range as an actor.

Just as *Easy Rider* had culminated the 1960s counterculture, *Five Easy Pieces* was the portent to the 1970s era of cinema filled with character studies, literate dialogue, and stylish direction. Special effects and different marketing strategies would obliterate this practice by the late 1970s with the box office success of *Jaws* (1975) and *Star Wars* (1977), but as the decade began, character-driven cinema became the norm. Nicholson's career would especially thrive due to his penchant for portraying quirky individuals who explored darker situations and confronted their own offbeat idiosyncrasies.

Nicholson once again received an Oscar nomination for *Five Easy Pieces*, this time for Best Actor. But this was the year of *Patton* as Best Picture, and that film's star, George C. Scott, was awarded a Best Actor Oscar, which he refused to accept. While the fact that Nicholson achieved Oscar nominations for his performances in *Easy Rider* and *Five Easy Pieces* was impressive at any level, the actor himself was unhappy with being a two-time loser at the Academy Awards. The film also lost its nominations for Best Picture, Best Original Screenplay, and Best Supporting Actress (Karen Black).

Older film critics who were slow to adapt to changing styles in cinema were often dismissive of movies that lacked a linear structure and a happy ending. Thus, it is not surprising that research reveals a review like Roger Greenspun's in the *New York Times*, which pontificates,

> I'm not sure how *Five Easy Pieces* will seem in retrospect—perhaps not all that good. Greater things seem always to be in the offing. But I think they are an illusion. *Five Easy Pieces* is a film that takes small risks and provides small rewards.[1]

However, critics eventually realized that *Five Easy Pieces* was a lasting and significant film. Roger Ebert stated on his website,

> *Five Easy Pieces* has the complexity, the nuance, the depth, of the best fiction. In involves us in these people, this time and place, and we care for them, even though they don't request our affection or applause. We remember Bobby and Rayette, because they are so completely themselves, so stuck, so needy, so brave in their loneliness. Once you have seen movie characters who are alive, it's harder to care about the robots in their puppet shows.[2]

Nicholson's other film releases in 1970 included a role in the Barbra Streisand vehicle *On a Clear Day You Can See Forever*—a film that was savaged by the critics—and the tardily released biker movie *Rebel Rousers*, which had been made a few years earlier, but came out in an attempt to capitalize on Nicholson's new fame. These films were pretty much ignored and did nothing to hamper or enhance his ever-growing status in American cinema.

CARNAL KNOWLEDGE

(1971, AVCO Embassy)

★ ★ ★ ★

Director: Mike Nichols
Screenplay: Jules Feiffer
Producer: Mike Nichols. *Cinematographer:* Giuseppe Rotunno. *Editor:* Sam
    O'Steen
Cast: Jack Nicholson (Jonathan Fuerst), Candice Bergen (Susan), Art
    Garfunkel (Sandy), Ann-Margret (Bobbie), Rita Moreno (Louise),
    Cynthia O'Neal (Cindy), Carol Kane (Jennifer)
Released: June 30, 1971
Specs: 98 minutes; Technicolor
Availability: DVD (MGM)

Just prior to the release of *Carnal Knowledge*, Jack Nicholson made his directorial debut with *Drive, He Said*, which was released about a month earlier. Nicholson did not act in the movie (other than a bearded cameo), and it was produced for Columbia by Raybert, the production company run by Bob Rafelson and Bert Schneider, who had scored with *Easy Rider* and *Five Easy Pieces*. Nicholson also wrote the screenplay for *Drive, He Said*, which deals with a college basketball star who dives into the sexual revolution with the same prowess as he exhibits on the basketball court (including an affair with the dean's wife). The film received mixed reviews, with Roger Ebert calling it both "disorganized" and "occasionally brilliant," adding, "Nicholson himself is a tremendously interesting screen actor, and he directs his actors to achieve a kind of intimacy and intensity that is genuinely rare. But if Nicholson is good on the nuances, he's weak on the overall direction of his film. It doesn't hang together for us as a unified piece of work."[1] Vincent Canby said the film was "so much better than all of the rest of the campus junk Hollywood has manufactured in the last couple of years."[2] The movie made little impact in its time and subsequently faded away, until a 2010 DVD release by Criterion, on the strength of the Nicholson name.

Carnal Knowledge was more prestigious and had a much stronger impact. Like *Drive, He Said*, it approaches the sexual revolution with frankness. However, unlike Nicholson's directorial debut, *Carnal Knowledge* is not initially about the sexual revolution. It is set in the late 1940s, the immediate postwar era where Americans attempt to cope with the country's prosperity after a depression and a world war, and how conservatism is being crowded by a postwar restlessness to which the pop culture responded with everything from James Dean to comic books to Elvis Presley. The sexuality that was hidden is examined in this Mike Nichols film as the characters grow from college students in the late forties to middle-agers in the early seventies, their sexual curiosity and growth occurring during the sexual revolution.

Nicholson's character of Jonathan has an aggressive approach to sexuality, being preoccupied with superficial externals like breast cup size, while Art Garfunkel's role of Jonathan's friend Sandy is more centered and seeks a meaningful relationship. The trajectory of their lives might take on different perspectives, but neither is happy by the time the film's setting reaches the present day. Jonathan continues to stumble from one experience to the other, shacking up with the equally sexual Bobbie, and the deeper affirmation she wants is never received. Sandy settles into a more conventional lifestyle but is at turns bored and bitter about his situation, speaking positively about it to Jonathan in an effort to fool himself into believing he is happier than he truly is.

Nicholson continues to envelope the quirkiness of his characters with Jonathan, another idiosyncratic, literate sort who cannot connect on a deeper level. There are elements of Bobby from *Five Easy Pieces*, the script allowing for Nicholson to explore the character's growth and maturity, and his both honing and reinventing his sexual perspective. And despite singer Garfunkel appearing in only his second film, his more passive character is not swallowed up by Nicholson's commanding performance. Ann-Margret is quite brilliant as Bobbie, recalling in her autobiography,

I'd met women like Bobbie Templeton, sensuous and fragile. Bobbie wants to marry and have children, but the man she is obsessed with, Jonathan, turns into a madman at the thought of surrendering his freedom.[3]

Candice Bergen, as the object of Sandy's affection, is, like Garfunkel, the more anchored character.

Carnal Knowledge is a very well-directed film, with Nichols making effective use of close-ups on the characters as they deliver their dialogue, sometimes speaking directly at the camera to the audience. Jules Feiffer's script offers some very witty exchanges. Feiffer initially didn't have faith in Nicholson's ability to play this character, but he changed his mind once he saw him acting in some of the more intense scenes. Each of the actors responds well to Nichols's intimate direction, and since Jonathan is the quirkiest and most unsettling character, it is Nicholson who comes off best. The scenes in which he and Ann-Margret confront each other with all of their emotional limitations, prejudicial shortcomings, failed expectations, and stubborn rigidity show off the best aspects of both actors' talent. Ann-Margret is no longer the giggly sex kitten with beauty and charisma; she is commanding in a layered role opposite Nicholson, who continues his growth as one of the breakout stars of the seventies. It's a bitter film, however, one that does seem to provide a portrait of the changing times as the sixties became the seventies.

While Nicholson was filming this movie, his triumph in *Easy Rider* was solidified, but his triumphant performance in *Five Easy Pieces* had not yet been released. However, by the time *Carnal Knowledge* came out, *Five Easy Pieces* made Nicholson's name as much responsible for the film's box office success as anyone, including producer-director Nichols. Film critic Roger Ebert stated,

> Nicholson, who is possibly the most interesting new movie actor since James Dean, carries the film, and his scenes with Ann-Margret are masterfully played.[4]

Carnal Knowledge was received with some controversy upon its release in 1971, as frank sexual discussion was hardly the norm. It is something of a benchmark that indicates how American cinema was changing and becoming a bit more free in its presentation of formerly taboo subjects. This was not as well received in some areas where the movie played. Police in Albany, Georgia, served a search warrant on a theater showing the movie, and seized the print from the projector. The theater manager was convicted of distributing obscene material. His conviction was upheld by the Supreme

Court of Georgia. However, the US Supreme Court found that the State of Georgia had gone too far in classifying material as obscene and overturned the conviction.

While Nicholson received a Golden Globe nomination for his performance, it was Ann-Margret who was nominated for an Oscar as well as a Golden Globe. Nicholson did not win his Golden Globe award. Ann-Margret did not win an Oscar. But she did win the Golden Globe. Unfortunately, the actress admitted in her autobiography that the film had an emotional impact on her that left in her in "a depressive stupor, fueled by drugs and alcohol."[5]

With *Carnal Knowledge*, Jack Nicholson had another critically acclaimed performance in release. He then appeared in Henry Jaglom's odd *A Safe Place* (1971) and reunited with Bob Rafelson for *The King of Marvin Gardens* (1972). The latter film has some minor interest, for Nicholson's role was originally offered to Al Pacino, while Nicholson at the same time had been offered Pacino's role in *The Godfather*. Each actor took the other's role as the respective director's second choice.

THE LAST DETAIL

(1973, Columbia)

★ ★ ★ ★ ★

Director: Hal Ashby
Screenplay: Robert Towne (based on the novel by Darryl Ponicsan)
Producer: Gerald Ayres. *Cinematographer:* Michael Chapman. *Editor:* Robert C.
    Jones
Cast: Jack Nicholson (Buddusky); Otis Young (Mulhall); Randy Quaid
    (Meadows); Clifton James (Chief Master-at-Arms); Michael Moriarty
    (Marine Duty Officer); Carol Kane (Young Whore); Luana Anders
    (Donna); Kathleen Miller (Annette); Nancy Allen (Nancy); Gerry
    Salsberg (Henry); Don McGovern (Bartender); Pat Hamilton
    (Madame); Michael Chapman (Taxi Driver); Jim Henshaw (Sweek);
    Derek McGrath, Gilda Radner, Jim Horn, John Castellano (Nichiren
    Shoshu Members); Henry Calvert (Pawnbroker)
Released: February 11, 1974
Specs: 104 minutes; Metrocolor
Availability: DVD (Columbia TriStar)

Jack Nicholson's critically acclaimed performances were consistent over several movies in which he was nominated for awards. He was now a proven talent in playing characters who were unconventional and whose idiosyncrasies he could exploit. In *The Last Detail*, his character of "Bad Ass" Buddusky is a series of contradictions. He is loyal to the US Navy, but disagrees with elements of the detail he is ordered to do. He is angry and volatile, but exhibits understanding and compassion. The character allows Nicholson to tap into a lot of the ideas he had tried in his first several movies, and convey the character's personality contradictions smoothly and effectively.

Buddusky and Mulhall are two navy men who are given five days to transport fellow sailor Meadows to a distant state where he must serve a prison sentence for stealing money from a charity. The charity happened to be one involving an officer's wife, so the sentence is especially severe: eight years in prison and a dishonorable discharge. Meadows turns out to be a shy, self-effacing, withdrawn young man of eighteen whose attempt at a petty theft has resulted in a severe sentence. He is confused and frightened, and doesn't quite know how to convey his feelings.

Buddusky is a career navy man who displays an edgy defiance but also maintains a firm and consistent loyalty to the service. And despite his initially distant response to Meadows, he can't help being softened by the naive midshipman's situation. Meadows is a virgin who has experienced little in his young life, and he is headed for a near-decade prison sentence that will keep him from these experiences even longer. Mulhall, another career navy man, and Buddusky have an understanding as to how to work

As navy man Buddusky in *The Last Detail. Columbia Pictures / Photofest © Columbia Pictures*

around military procedure and still complete their assignment. They agree to use the full five days they have to transport Meadows and show him a good time. Their journey, then, is filled with drinking, fighting, women, hotel rooms, and bars. Throughout these sequences, Mulhall and Buddusky learn more about their prisoner, get to like him as a buddy, but still realize they must do their duty.

Each of the three lead actors approaches his character brilliantly. Otis Young, an African American actor, does not essentially play a "black character" in the traditional sense. He simply plays a character who is a significant part of the film. It is a role that could have been played by an actor of any race or heritage. Young was, at the time of this film, a ten-year veteran of movies and TV, including a one-season stint starring on the ABC series *The Outsiders*. He plays Mulhall as his own man, not one who merely goes along with Buddusky's plans. He is part of the planning. The use of black actors in nonstereotypical roles was still building rather gradually even as late as 1972. Young's is a standout performance.

Randy Quaid was a newcomer to films when he essayed the Meadows role, having only been active for about two years.[1] Quaid effectively balances his performance from the shy, withdrawn sailor that Meadows is at the beginning of the film to the bolder, more confident man he becomes after spending days and nights in the company of the more experienced Buddusky and Mulhall. Even a simple bit where he refuses to send back a cheeseburger that he is served, with Buddusky having to intervene, is significant. Later in the movie, Meadows argues with the waiter that his eggs are not cooked over medium as ordered, while Buddusky looks on proudly.

With this role, Nicholson continued to display his range as an actor. His expression usually alternates between defiance and weariness, accepting the detail and planning to carry it out without connecting to the prisoner or his situation. But almost immediately after he meets Meadows, Buddusky's eyes soften as he watches the young midshipman weep over his situation. Rather than dismiss the younger sailor's emotional response, he shows compassion that is hard-edged but not begrudging.

Robert Towne's profanity-laced script is authentic to Darryl Ponicsan's novel, and in 1973, this sort of dialogue was still shocking.[2] It helps to define the characters, especially Nicholson's, whose volatility is often displayed via four-letter words. Hal Ashby is the perfect director for this film; his progressive sensibilities and understanding of defiance to authority and the counterculture assist in making the film's point. Meadows is guilty for a petty crime. His crime does not deserve an eight-year prison sentence. Both Mulhall and Buddusky realize that the young sailor is being given harsher treatment because his petty theft directly involved a charity headed by an officer's wife. The detail becomes more and more difficult for them emotionally as they proceed and get to know Meadows. Throughout the movie, no matter how much fun they are having, it is not enough to completely distract any of them. At one point Mulhall and Buddusky are sitting on a park bench in the snow with Meadows out of earshot, when an uncomfortable Mulhall says, "Let's just get this over with." It is beautifully shot by Ashby, who has the camera closing in on the actors, framing them with the bleakness of the snowy background.

There are several interesting details to the proceedings. A visit to a whorehouse to allow Meadows his first sexual experience is shown as a cheap, dirty environment where the women are not particularly attractive at all. Meadows chooses the best-looking one. A dull, uneventful party with three women ends with the sailors' confused reaction to the girls' politics and their penchant for meditation. Throughout these tangential stops along the way, Buddusky and Mulhall continue to realize their duty and expect to fulfill it, while Meadows tries to bury his fear about his destination. Most of the time, the three are laughing and carrying on. But, periodically, they stop and ponder just what it is they're doing. "They'll knock off two years right away," Buddusky tells Meadows in an attempt to reassure him, "so you really only have six." This thought is, at least, marginal help to Meadows's plight, and he brings it up whenever his sentence is discussed, which helps us to understand both Meadows's desperation and Buddusky's forceful ability to influence the younger sailor.

Perhaps the most interesting sequences involve two different situations where Meadows attempts to escape. The first one is impulsive and happens on the train almost immediately after he is placed in the custody of Mulhall and Buddusky. It is simply a frightened reaction, and he is quickly apprehended. The second occurs as the three are closer to their destination and have been through several experiences together. Meadows, standing a distance away from the other two, uses signals to indicate he is running away and does so. He is eventually captured and beaten by Buddusky, who feels oddly betrayed by the action. Meadows had been entrusted to make the journey without handcuffs; he was given beer, warm places to sleep, a sexual experience, and other distractions during the five-day excursion, which was treated more as a liberty than part of an assignment to transport a man to prison. His attempted escape toward the end of the movie seems abrupt and jarring, even more so than the impulsive action earlier. When they finally arrive at their destination, a weeping Meadows is taken away to his cell without any goodbyes. As the two other men are walking away from the situation, Mulhall says to Buddusky, "I hated this chicken shit detail."

The creation of *The Last Detail* was not without incident. Nicholson was committed to the film *The King of Marvin Gardens*, so production stalled for eighteen months while he filmed that movie. Producer Ayers and director Ashby used that time to scout locations, interview servicemen, and tighten the script. Jack Nicholson wanted his old friend Rupert Crosse from the Monte Hellman movies to play Mulhall, and Hal Ashby, who had final say in casting, accepted this request. However, Crosse was diagnosed with terminal cancer just as production began. Production was suspended, and he was given a week to deal with this news, but he then decided that he would be unable to do the movie. He died in March 1973. Otis Young turned in perhaps the finest performance of his career in the role. Ashby was busted for marijuana possession while scouting locations in Canada, and almost lost the project as a result, but Nicholson intervened, insisting that Ashby direct. Nicholson would later recall, "Hal is the first director to let me go, to let me find my own level."[3]

The Last Detail is an example of "the new Hollywood" that began in the late 1960s when a film like *Bonnie and Clyde* (1967) gave 1930s gangsters 1960s wild-child sensibilities, and when *The Graduate* (1967) looked specifically at the current era's American youth and how their perspective as they transitioned to adulthood differed from that of the previous generation. *The Last Detail* also shows us the military without the sort of movie matinee bravado found in earlier dramas. Made during the waning days of the Vietnam War, when reaction by some young people to servicemen was negative, *The Last Detail* shows us a military situation that is unsettling without being set on the battlefield. Other characters challenge the status of the two career navy men. When Mulhall is asked by a young woman why he went to Vietnam, he simply and matter-of-factly responds that was what he was ordered to do ("what the man says"). The woman is so shocked by his complacent attitude, she is unable to respond other than to slowly shake her head and say, "Wow." This was a transitional period, and Hal Ashby's counterculture perspective was an effective framework not only for Nicholson's iconoclastic character, but also for the setting and each situation. It is as if Mulhall and Buddusky are in a prison of their own, that prison being the navy. They're fiercely loyal to it, but I got the feeling that they don't really know why they are loyal and that they keep feeling compelled to do things they don't think are right—like taking Meadows to prison.

The Last Detail held its New York premiere in late December 1973, but its wide release was not until the following February. Vincent Canby, in his *New York Times* review, stated,

> *The Last Detail* is one superbly funny, uproariously intelligent performance, plus two others that are very, very good, which are so effectively surrounded by profound bleakness that it seems to be a new kind of anti-comedy. It's a good movie but an unhomogenized one. Mr. Nicholson dominates the film with what amounts to an anthology of swaggers optimistic, knowing, angry, foolish and forlorn. It's by far the best thing he's ever done. If anything it's almost too good in that it disguises with charm the empty landscape of the life it represents.[4]

The Last Detail cost $2.6 million to make and grossed $10 million domestically.[5] The film was nominated for the Palme d'Or at the 1974 Cannes Film Festival, and Nicholson was awarded Best Actor. Nicholson was also nominated for a Best Actor Academy Award, as was Randy Quaid for Best Supporting Actor and Robert Towne for Best Writing, Screenplay Based on Material from Another Medium. Nicholson and Quaid were also nominated for Golden Globes. Nicholson won Best Actor awards from the National Society of Film Critics and the New York Film Critics Circle.

Learning his craft in the low-budget movies, establishing himself as a star in *Easy Rider*, becoming a bankable box office attraction with *Five Easy Pieces* and *Carnal* Knowledge, Jack Nicholson was now an award-winning top-level superstar with *The Last Detail*. However, Nicholson was never one to simply rest on his laurels. Although he had been in movies for more than fifteen years by the time of *The Last Detail*, Nicholson was still in the period where he wanted to explore different roles and try different concepts, rather than rest within the comfortable trappings of a consistent screen persona. In his continuing quest to stretch as an actor and investigate new ideas, Jack Nicholson next explored film noir in Roman Polanski's *Chinatown*.

CHINATOWN

(1974, Paramount)

★ ★ ★ ★ ★

Director: Roman Polanski
Screenplay: Robert Towne
Producer: Robert Evans. *Cinematographer:* John A. Alonzo. *Editor:* Sam O'Steen
Cast: Jack Nicholson (J. J. Gittes), Faye Dunaway (Evelyn Mulwray), John
    Huston (Noah Cross), Perry Lopez (Escobar), John Hillerman
    (Yelburton), Darrell Zwerling (Hollis Mulwray), Diane Ladd (Ida
    Sessions), Roy Jensen (Mulvihill), Roman Polanski (Man with Knife),
    Dick Bakalyan (Loach), Joe Mantell (Walsh), Bruce Glover (Duffy),
    Nandu Hinds (Sophie), James O'Rear (Lawyer), James Hong (Butler),
    Beulah Quo (Maid), Jerry Fujikawa (Gardener), Belinda Palmer
    (Katherine), Roy Roberts (Bagby), Noble Willingham (Councilman),
    Rance Howard (Farmer), Jesse Vint (Farmer), Burt Young (Curly),
    Elizabeth Harding (Curly's Wife), Charles Knapp (Mortician), Elliot
    Montgomery (Councilman)
Released: June 20, 1974
Specs: 130 minutes; Technicolor
Availability: DVD (Paramount)

One of the strongest films in Jack Nicholson's long career, *Chinatown* is a triumph for everyone involved in its production. Robert Towne turned in a script that is filled with smart dialogue, well-drawn characters, and a narrative that continues to reveal fascinating details. Roman Polanski's basing his directorial vision on traditional film noir elements is both artistically clever and aesthetically rewarding. And the performances, from the smallest roles to the largest, are relentless and brilliant. With this film Jack Nicholson continues to establish himself as among the finest screen actors of his time.

The mainstream pop culture of the 1970s had been enjoying a nostalgia craze that started around 1968 and continued till the middle of the 1970s. College campuses celebrated the films of Humphrey Bogart, the Marx Brothers, W. C. Fields, and other subversive characters of vintage cinema, believing them to be the portent to their own counterculture perspective. With his direction of *Chinatown*, Roman Polanski taps into that interest in nostalgia by crafting a 1940s film noir prototype, set in 1937, with appropriately atmospheric music, dark imagery, lingering close-ups, and a set design that frames each scene with careful authenticity.

Jack Nicholson stars as Jake Gittes, the sort of quintessential shady private detective that had been epitomized in 1940s films by the likes of Bogart

As private detective J. J. Gittes in Roman Polanski's neo-noir *Chinatown*. *Paramount Pictures / Photofest © Paramount Pictures*

or Alan Ladd. A woman claiming to be the wife asks Gittes to trail Water Commissioner Hollis Mulwray, on suspicion that he is cheating on her. Mr. Mulwray is soon found dead, and Gittes discovers the real Mrs. Mulwray is someone else entirely—the daughter of Noah Cross, a powerful businessman who is controlling the water in Los Angeles, directing it to his orchards. As Gittes further unravels the layers that surround the corruption, he discovers personal secrets about both Mrs. Mulwray and Mr. Cross. As with most detective mysteries that use this narrative structure, Gittes is soon mired so deeply into the situation he's investigating, it is difficult to find his way out.

The eeriness of his surroundings is not lost on Gittes. He has this exchange with Evelyn Mulwray:

Evelyn Mulwray: Tell me, Mr. Gittes: Does this often happen to you?

Jake Gittes: What's that?

Evelyn: Well, I'm judging only on the basis of one afternoon and an evening, but, uh, if this is how you go about your work, I'd say you'd be lucky to, uh, get through a whole day.

Jake: Actually, this hasn't happened to me for a long time.

Evelyn: When was the last time?

Jake: Why?

Evelyn: It's an innocent question.

Jake: In Chinatown.

Evelyn: What were you doing there?

Jake: Working for the district attorney.

Evelyn: Doing what?

Jake: As little as possible.

Evelyn: The district attorney gives his men advice like that?

Jake: They do in Chinatown.

Screenwriter Robert Towne reportedly studied actual 1930s cases of corruption in Los Angeles to inspire his brilliant Oscar-winning script. But the character of Jake Gittes was written for Jack Nicholson. Nicholson stated in an interview with Josh Horowitz at MTV.com,

I actually never think it works when somebody writes for me. It doesn't leave me enough room to move. But I didn't think that way that far back. I just liked it because it was a departure from most films. It was a detective with no gun.[1]

The compelling script derives from a series of situations driven by dialogue. And it is the natural quality of the dialogue that defines each character. When Gittes confronts Noah Cross, he is taken aback at anyone having such massive wealth.

Jake Gittes: How much are you worth?

Noah Cross: I have no idea. How much do you want?

Jake: I just wanna know what you're worth. More than 10 million?

Noah: Oh my, yes!

Jake: Why are you doing it? How much better can you eat? What could you buy that you can't already afford?

Noah: You see, Mr. Gittes, most people never have to face the fact that at the right time and the right place, they're capable of anything.

At the time, Roman Polanski was living in France, and despite having been friends with Nicholson since the 1960s and interested in working with him, he was not interested in returning to America to work, as it was less than ten years since his pregnant wife, Sharon Tate, and several friends were brutally murdered by the Manson family. Polanski was attracted to Towne's script upon reading it, being especially impressed with how layered each character was. However, according to his biography, Polanski had some misgivings as to the depth of the project, realizing it could not effectively be filmed without some rewriting. Towne made extensive rewrites, cutting some characters out all together and changing what was originally a happy ending. Polanski believed, and correctly, that a shocking, downer ending would be more effective. So Towne's original version, where Noah Cross dies, was changed to the surprising death of Mrs. Mulwray as the film concludes. Producer Robert Evans supported this darker version, as that was the chief reason he had chosen to use a European director for this project. He believed the more cynical vision from a director with a background and experience in European cinema would benefit the project. Towne's script is complex, and a less skilled director could have lapsed into melodrama during some of the later, more emotional scenes.

One especially shocking sequence is the scene where Jake confronts Evelyn as he gradually starts to reach some conclusions about her relationship with her father. He wants her to admit the truth as to her connection to Katherine, who is also identified as her sister. Evelyn shouts, "She's my daughter!" and is slapped. Gittes continues to demand the truth. Evelyn claims, "She's my sister" and is slapped again. Finally, after a few more similar exchanges, Evelyn admits, "She's my sister and my daughter!" Her incestuous relationship with Noah Cross is revealed. This scene is shocking not only for its content, but also for the way Dunaway and Nicholson play it. It is pure tension, and each slap cracks like a whip. As Gittes becomes more forceful, Evelyn becomes more submissive.

The casting of noted director John Huston in a rare acting role as Noah Cross offers another connection to past film noir. Huston made his directorial debut with *The Maltese Falcon* (1941), a vintage noir prototype that advanced Humphrey Bogart from character actor to top-drawer leading man. Huston plays Cross as a man confident and settled due to his immense wealth. He is capable of controlling situations without scruples, never being taken to task for his layers of illegal activity, despite Gittes's pleas to police as he discovers more about Cross's sordid ways. Nicholson does not play the central detective character in the classic noir tradition. This is an update with a more modern perspective set within the parameters of classic noir. Nicholson plays Gittes as more edgy than measured, responding effectively to areas within the seamy underbelly of society that past films could not explore. Nicholson was in a relationship with Huston's daughter, actress Anjelica, at this time, and recalled for Josh Horowitz,

> It was one of the great privileges of my life to be around John Huston. He was, of course, a father figure to me. I loved him to death.[2]

There are a lot of similarities between Sam Spade in *The Maltese Falcon* and Jake Gittes in *Chinatown*. Both detectives are drawn into what initially appears to be a simple case that quickly grows in complexity. There is a lot of Bogart's method of playing a character in Nicholson's performance as well, while Dunaway evokes the classic femme fatale perfectly. Both are grittier than 1940s noir, as the seventies allowed much more freedom in presentation than the earlier movies. It's rare to see film set in a past era that actually feels like it could have been made in that era, while remaining contemporary. *Chinatown* manages to convey this impressively.

It is easy for the audience to identify with Gittes because Polanski shot the film from this character's perspective. We progress through the story with Gittes, learn things as he learns them, and at times even see exactly what he's seeing, through binoculars or a mirror, as in a scene where he trails Mr. Mulwray. It's an effective technique that builds suspense while also ensuring the audience's involvement.

Chinatown is dotted with strong character actors in smaller roles, including the welcome, familiar faces of Burt Young, James Hong, John Hillerman, Diane Ladd, Bruce Glover, and Roy Roberts. In one scene, Gittes has his nose sliced by a knife-wielding henchman, played by director Roman Polanski in a chilling, effective cameo. Nicholson plays a good portion of the film with his face obscured by a bandage. Critics pointed out the courage of a leading man obscuring his face for the body of the movie, and still able to convey the emotional strength necessary.

The film's conclusion continues with this tension as Evelyn tries to drive away with her daughter, and a pawing and pleading Noah Cross trying to wrest some sort of control. The girl is both confused and frightened. Evelyn pulls out a gun, shooting Cross in the arm. She drives away, but police open fire. Evelyn is killed, and Cross leads the hysterical daughter away, while Jake protests. One of his associates says, "Forget it, Jake. It's Chinatown," which is the film's closing line.

Critics were unanimous in their praise for this feature. Vincent Canby stated in the *New York Times*, "Mr. Nicholson wears an air of comic, lazy, very vulnerable sophistication that is this film's major contribution to the genre,"[3] while Roger Ebert in the *Chicago Sun-Times* wrote that Nicholson "inhabits the character of J.J. Gittes like a second skin; the possession is so total that there are scenes in the movie where we almost have telepathy; we know what he's thinking, so he doesn't have to tell us."[4] Critic James Berardinelli stated on the ReelViews website,

> At first glance, Jake Gittes (Nicholson) seems like the kind of private investigator who would be at home in the pages of a Dashiel Hammett or Raymond Chandler novel. In fact, when we first encounter Gittes, we can almost see the shadow of Humphrey Bogart occupying his space. But that's an illusion. As we come to learn, Gittes isn't as thick-skinned as his numerous predecessors. He cares (a decided rarity amongst the cynical lot that are cinematic P.I.'s) and lives his life by a series of moral precepts that are not always governed by the principle of self-interest. Sure, Gittes can trade one-liners with the best of them, but his heart is bigger, and beats louder, than any of them. . . . This movie shows off multiple facets of (Nicholson's) talent—tenderness, quiet intensity, bulldog tenacity, and bravery in the face of danger. This film, his first lead role, changed the direction of his career.[5]

From a budget of $6 million, *Chinatown* grossed nearly $30 million in its 1974 initial domestic release. It was nominated for eleven Oscars, including the performances of Jack Nicholson and Faye Dunaway, neither of whom won. Robert Towne's screenplay was the only Academy Award recipient.

Towne had turned down $175,000 to write the screenplay for *The Great Gatsby* (believing he couldn't do cinematic justice to the Fitzgerald novel), and instead took $25,000 to write *Chinatown*. His script has since become championed as one of the finest examples of screenwriting in modern American cinema. Carson Reeves stated on the *ScriptShadow* blog,

> If you polled every established screenwriter in the business and asked them what the best screenplay ever written was, *Chinatown* would probably come out on top. The Robert Towne screenplay is considered to be the gold standard of screenwriting.[6]

The story was supposed to be a trilogy, and a second film, *The Two Jakes*, was produced in 1990. Towne wrote the script, and Nicholson starred and directed, but *The Two Jakes* failed at the box office. At a budget of nearly $20 million, *The Two Jakes* took in only about half that amount at the box office. Thus, no third film was made.

One of the oddest incidents to occur while Nicholson was doing publicity for *Chinatown* was an interview with *Time* magazine for a cover story called "The Star with the Killer Smile." The interviewer revealed that he found, in his research, that the people who raised Nicholson as his parents were actually his grandparents, while the ones he knew as his sisters were, in fact, his mother and his aunt. This revelation was difficult and confusing for the actor on a personal level, and it helped shape further performances as his characters became increasingly more of the nature of those who had "seen it all" and were perversely amused by their off-kilter surroundings.

⑬

ONE FLEW OVER THE CUCKOO'S NEST

(1975, United Artists)

★ ★ ★ ★ ★

Director: Miloš Forman
Screenplay: Lawrence Hauben, Bo Goldman, based on the novel by Ken
    Kesey. *Play adaptation:* Dale Wasserman
Producers: Michael Douglas, Saul Zaentz. *Cinematographers:* Haskell Wexler,
    Bill Butler (uncredited). *Editors:* Sheldon Kahn, Lynzee Klingman
Cast: Jack Nicholson (R. P. McMurphy), Louise Fletcher (Nurse Ratched),
    Brad Dourif (Billy Bibbit), Will Sampson (Chief), Christopher Lloyd
    (Taber), Scatman Crothers (Turkle), Sydney Lassick (Cheswick),
    William Redfield (Harding), Michael Berryman (Ellis), Vincent Schiavelli
    (Fredrickson), Alonzo Brown (Miller), Mwako Cumbuka (Warren),
    Danny DeVito (Martini), William Duell (Jim Sefelt), Josip Elic (Bancini),
    Lan Fendors (Nurse Itsu), Peter Brocco (Col. Matterson), Dean
    R. Brooks (Dr. Spivey), Nathan George (Washington), Phil Roth
    (Woolsey), Louisa Moritz (Rose), Marya Small (Candy), Ken Kenny
    (Beans), Mimi Sarkisian (Nurse Pilbow), Delos Smith (Scanlon), Mel
    Lambert (Habor Master)
Released: November 21, 1975
Specs: 133 minutes; color
Availability: DVD (Warner Home Video)

By *Chinatown*, Nicholson had already achieved leading man status, and with *One Flew over the Cuckoo's Nest*, he reached the level of icon. His performance in this film was so layered, filled with so many disparate elements of personality, and conveyed so expertly that Jack Nicholson became among the most highly regarded symbols of the acting profession thereafter.

The story behind *One Flew over the Cuckoo's Nest* is interesting and varied. Back in 1963, Kirk Douglas, still hot off his performance in Stanley Kubrick's *Spartacus* (1962), bought the rights to Ken Kesey's 1962 novel. He wanted to produce the property and play the character of McMurphy. He bought the rights for $47,000 but couldn't find any backers to finance a movie version. Cinema was a lot more conservative in 1962, and a story like this would not fit comfortably among such films as *Lawrence of Arabia*, *To Kill a Mockingbird*, and *The Music Man*. Douglas then decided to produce it as a play. He believed if it was successful on Broadway, he could more easily generate interest in a film version. The play opened on Broadway in November 1963, but with little success, closing by the following January.

After spending another dozen unsuccessful years trying to get a film version made, Kirk Douglas then offered to sell the rights for $150,000 to anyone who wanted them. Nobody did. Fed up, Kirk gave the rights to his son Michael, who hoped to at least get back his father's original investment. The younger Douglas also had a hard time securing interest until hooking up with Saul Zaentz, a music producer who earlier had some interest in the property while Kirk Douglas still had the rights. Zaentz and Michael Douglas commissioned a script from original novelist Kesey, but it was disappointing, as Kesey could not make an effective transition to screenwriting, which is a different approach entirely. Bo Goldman was then hired to do a complete rewrite, while Douglas secured the services of Miloš Forman as director and arranged for Jack Nicholson to play the role of McMurphy. This was after such actors as Marlon Brando, Gene Hackman, Burt Reynolds, and James Caan had all turned the role down and after Hal Ashby passed on the directing. Kirk Douglas was of the understanding that he would still play the role, and it fell to son Michael to gently inform his father that he was now too old for the part.

Upon completing *Chinatown*, Jack Nicholson had appeared in the film version of the Who's rock opera *Tommy* (1975) and played opposite Warren Beatty in Mike Nichols's funny yet decidedly disappointing 1920s-era comedy *The Fortune* (1975). While these average films were well received in some quarters, neither did much to capitalize on the leading man status that Nicholson had established with *Chinatown*.

One interesting performance Nicholson did offer after *Chinatown* and before *One Flew over the Cuckoo's Nest* was in Michelangelo Antonioni's atmospheric *The Passenger* (1975), which benefited from the director's vision and Luciono Tovoli's camerawork. But while it enjoyed strong critical acclaim and has lived on as one of the director's more interesting films, it did little to generate further interest in Jack Nicholson's career at the time. It remains one of his best performances during this period. Nicholson's role in *One Flew over the Cuckoo's Nest* surpasses both *Chinatown* and *The Passenger*, and may be the finest performance of his career.

Nicholson stars as Randall Patrick McMurphy, a thirty-eight-year-old patient who is confined to a mental institution due to his uncontrollable behavior on a work farm, where he was sent for statutory rape. McMurphy is at times manic and tumultuous and at other times controlled and seemingly intelligent. In fact, the penitentiary that sent him to the institution noted that McMurphy might be faking mental instability in order to get out of his work detail. The institution is to evaluate him.

Nicholson conveys the character's complexities immediately. As soon as McMurphy's handcuffs are removed, he starts yelling and jumps on one of the guards and kisses him. He dances in front of a mute Indian chief at one point, and soon afterward is answering interview questions with a witty lucidity. When the doctor points out that he engaged in eight fights while at the work farm, McMurphy responds, "Archie Moore has forty and you don't lock him up." McMurphy is an observer as much as he is a participant. He is quietly bemused during a monitored discussion session when an argument, not involving him, breaks out, and the various emotional disabilities of each patient are displayed. But he has natural leadership abilities. He attempts to teach basketball to the mute Native American, whom he has nicknamed Chief. He tries to teach a group of patients how to play poker, but succumbs to frustration when they fail to grasp the concept of the game. His enthusiasm is infectious at times; he is obviously a character who loves life and tries to impart that to the other inmates.

It is not long before the narrative establishes a conflict between McMurphy and Nurse Ratched, the unsmiling manager of the patients who dispenses their medication and rules over them. She is quiet, reserved, but firm and unfeeling. McMurphy immediately perceives her as the enemy, while the others are terrified of her. He attempts politeness when asking if the patients can watch the World Series. She puts it to a vote, but despite his leadership skills, McMurphy can't get enough of the others to vote against the wishes of the nurse.

Randall Patrick McMurphy (Nicholson) confronts Nurse Ratched (Louise Fletcher) in *One Flew over the Cuckoo's Nest. United Artists / Photofest © United Artists*

Of course, the World Series is several days long, so McMurphy attempts the same thing the next day. More hands are raised, enough for a majority, but the nurse does not honor the victory. She indicates that the nine men in the group do not count, as there are eighteen patients in the ward. The problem is, the other nine are serious cases that don't understand the situation. McMurphy goes to each one, passionately trying to get another vote. He finally gets Chief to respond, but the nurse has ended the meeting and refuses to count Chief's vote. McMurphy responds by creating the game himself, putting on an impromptu performance by acting as a baseball announcer: "Koufax pitches. It's a fly ball to left center, it's going, it's gone!" His charisma is enough to attract the others, who crowd around him and cheer as if watching an actual game.

This scene is not only one of the highlights of *One Flew over the Cuckoo's Nest*, it is one of the most stirring, emotionally uplifting, and brilliantly executed scenes in the history of American cinema. Nicholson's bravura performance in this scene alone likely solidified the Oscar he would later win for the role.

As an observer, McMurphy notices the problems of each inmate and the control Nurse Ratched has over each. Without trying, McMurphy's leadership skills start to influence the others. Some of them begin to question her authority, and feel tentative courage toward her control of their situations. The inmates also begin to form a friendly allegiance to McMurphy. They feel more and more comfortable with his authority. This is especially borne out in a scene where McMurphy enlists Chief's help, climbs atop his shoulders, and goes over the barbed wire fence. McMurphy hides in a bus in which the patients are about to take a field trip, and when the others board, he drives away and they go on a boat ride. Structurally, this scene distracts from the narrative, causing it to change direction. Director Miloš Forman didn't want to use the scene, but Nicholson talked him into it. As it turns out, Nicholson's instincts were correct. The scene further establishes McMurphy's relationship with the others, and shows how they function much more effectively with him than they do in the confines of the institution and under the hard rule of Nurse Ratched. Their excitement when two of the patients get a fish on their line and the triumph of their successfully reeling in two big marlins make whatever trouble they get into upon sailing in and being brought back worthwhile.

McMurphy's conflict with the nurse and his leadership of the other patients are further embellished by his relationship with Chief. When McMurphy enlists the very tall man's help in his escape, Forman cuts to a close-up of Chief smiling, letting us know that his brain waves are not so limited as he lets on. This ominous foreshadowing is gradually revealed further during another basketball game, where Chief is able to respond to the game, blocking the shots of others, and dunking the ball into the basket when it's passed to him. When a disruption in another group meeting results in both McMurphy and Chief being given shock treatment, Chief reveals himself to his friend as they wait. Thanking him verbally for the gum he shares, Chief then admits to McMurphy that he can speak, hear, and think. "Let's get out of here," McMurphy says. It is a plan they both agree to make when the time is right.

Character actors of some note round out the smaller parts that help frame McMurphy's central role: Brad Dourif, in his Oscar-nominated role of the stuttering Billy Bibbit, whose fear of Nurse Ratched stems from the same fear he has of his overbearing mother; Sydney Lassick as the meek, frightened Cheswick, who discovers a reserve of courage due to McMurphy's towering influence; and other, even more familiar actors like Christopher Lloyd, Danny DeVito, and Scatman Crothers (as a harried nighttime orderly) all help expand the narrative while the focus remains on Nicholson. Most of these actors were unknowns at the time of filming.

The film concludes after McMurphy has accomplished his greatest defiance of authority. He enlists the cooperation of the overnight orderly, and soon there are hookers and booze in the ward. The patients respond favorably until McMurphy and Chief plan to leave with the women. McMurphy idealistically allows Bibbit to enjoy a sexual encounter with one of the girls, but the boozing and partying puts them all to sleep and they're lying there the next morning. McMurphy has missed his chance. Nurse Ratched and the nighttime orderlies discover the disarray. Billy Bibbit comes out of his room and his stuttering is gone. The sexual release has also released whatever inhibitions have affected his speech and manner. However, when Nurse Ratched indicates she is going to tell his mother, Billy's stuttering returns even more heavily, as he begs her not to do so. Moments later, he is found dead, having sliced his own throat. McMurphy, in a fit of rage, tries to strangle Nurse Ratched. For punishment, he is lobotomized. Chief weeps when the catatonic McMurphy returns to the ward and smothers him with a pillow to put him out of his misery. Chief then uses his brute strength to throw a heavy object through a window (an object McMurphy couldn't budge earlier in the film) and escapes. The last shot is him running away in the darkness.

Will Sampson's portrayal of Chief is perhaps the highlight of the actor's career, and it is in his film debut. When he is playing Chief as deaf and dumb, he stares straight ahead, not letting us know he is listening and absorbing all around him. His smile when McMurphy gets over the fence is one of understanding and admiration. His eventual coming out of his shell is because of McMurphy's attention and influence. When he has to kill his friend, putting him out of his misery, it is after a brilliantly played moment where Chief goes to McMurphy's bed and excitedly tries to rekindle their plans to escape. His face slowly falls into sadness as he realizes McMurphy has been lobotomized.

The film is based on a 1962 novel, a time when procedures such as shock treatments and lobotomies were sadly common practices that, over time, have been jettisoned. The film, then, is not as much an indictment of those methods, as the earlier book might have been, but a nostalgic throwback to an era where such procedures did take place. The consistent string that maintains throughout the film's narrative is that these patients are as much responding to their environment and treatment as they are to their own clinical diagnosis. This is borne out by their behavior when under McMurphy's guidance versus their reaction to the structure implemented by Nurse Ratched.

Louise Fletcher, who plays Ratched, won an Oscar, as did Nicholson, director Forman, and screenwriters Bo Goldman and Lawrence Hauben, while the film also garnered the Academy Award for Best Picture. It was the first film since Frank Capra's *It Happened One Night* (1934) to take all of the major Academy Awards. Forman believed Louise Fletcher was all wrong for the role, but he realized when she read for him that there was the necessary toughness he wanted for the character. His instincts were correct. Fletcher plays the role brilliantly, conveying the sort of smug control and vindictive, uncaring personality that define the character of Ratched. However, by the end of production, Louise Fletcher had become so weary of playing a character so tight lipped and straight laced that during a break as production was concluding, she ripped off her costume and stood in her panties to prove to the others that she was not the cold-hearted monster that she was portraying. Fletcher told Aljean Hametz in a 1975 interview,

> Everybody else had too much to do. . . . When you're being crazy, the sky is the limit. I envied the other actors tremendously. They were so free, and I had to be so controlled. I was so totally frustrated that I had the only tantrum I've ever had in my whole life outside the confines of my own house. The still photographer kept taking pictures of all the crazies and putting them up in the hospital dining room. I asked why he didn't take pictures of me and he said, "You're so boring, always in that white uniform." With 6-year-old bitchiness, I went into the dining room and tore down the few pictures he had taken of me.[1]

In his review, Vincent Canby said,

> As played by Louise Fletcher and defined in the screenplay by Lawrence Hauben and Bo Goldman, the film's Nurse Ratched is a much more interesting, more ambiguous character than in Mr. Kesey's novel, though what we take to be her fleeting impulses of genuine concern only make the film's ending that much more unbelievable.[2]

One Flew over the Cuckoo's Nest was shot on location at an Oregon institution, with director Forman using actual doctors and patients as extras. To prepare for his role, Nicholson took the method actor's approach and tried to connect with the actual inmates in an asylum. He ate with them, talked with them, and studied them. Filming began in January 1975 and continued into April. Once production completed, Nicholson had a hard time leaving the role behind, as he had connected with some of the actual inmates who appeared as extras. Director Miloš Forman's vision was aided by the great cinematography of Haskell Wexler. Forman recalled in an interview for the Director's Guild of America,

> We had maximum two cameras on the set, and even then it was a struggle, because I was working with Haskell Wexler—one of the greatest cameramen of all time, but a perfectionist. I would have scenes in which I would want one camera to concentrate on the actor who was the focus of the scene and another to just wander around among all the other faces, without telling the actors when they were on. That was very difficult for Haskell. He'd say, "I can't light everybody perfectly." But on the set you can only have one perfectionist, either the director or the cameraman, not both. Because, you know, the ideal shot for a cameraman is without actors. When there's nothing moving, the shot can be lit perfectly.[3]

Nicholson, however, did not get along well with Forman. In many cases the two would communicate through crew members and avoid speaking to each other.

When *One Flew over the Cuckoo's Nest* was released, the film was met with unanimous critical acclaim. Author Kesey, however, was unhappy that his own script was completely rewritten and refused to see the film. He also was dissatisfied with the casting of Nicholson in the lead (he wanted Gene Hackman) and that Chief did not narrate the movie in a voiceover as he narrates the book.

After his success in *One Flew over the Cuckoo's Nest*, Nicholson then went into Arthur Penn's western *The Missouri Breaks* (1976). While it could be argued in some respects that a film teaming Jack Nicholson and Marlon Brando would be essential within the filmography of either actor, *The Missouri Breaks* is not. This overlong, bloated feature boasted their teaming and, thus, should have been much better. Nicholson was paid $1.25 million for ten weeks' work, plus 10 percent of the gross in excess of $12.5 million. The domestic box office for *The Missouri Breaks* was only $14 million. Believing the film would flop, Nicholson sold back 5 percent of the eventual gross to the producer for a million dollars. He agreed, but the money was not forthcoming, forcing Nicholson to sue.

Nicholson followed this misfire with an equally disappointing screen version of F. Scott Fitzgerald's *The Last Tycoon* (1976), which boasted a cast that included Robert De Niro, Tony Curtis, Robert Mitchum, Donald Pleasence, and Jeanne Moreau and direction by Elia Kazan from a script by Harold Pinter. *The Last Tycoon* lost nearly $4 million at the box office. It was not until 1978 that Nicholson made another movie, and this time he would both star and direct.

GOIN' SOUTH

(1978, Paramount)

★ ★ ★

Director: Jack Nicholson
Screenplay: John Herman Shaner, Al Ramrus, Charles Shyer, Alan Mandel
Producers: Harry Gittes, Harold Schneider. *Cinematographer:* Nestor
    Almendros. *Editor:* John Fitzgerald Beck
Cast: Jack Nicholson (Henry Moon), Mary Steenburgen (Julia Tate),
    Christopher Lloyd (Towfield), John Belushi (Hector), Veronica
    Cartwright (Hermine), Danny DeVito (Hog), Tracey Walter (Coogan),
    Gerald H. Reynolds (Polty), Luana Anders (Lorette), George W. Smith
    (Mr. Anderson), Lucy Lee Flippin (Diane), Ed Begley Jr. (Whitey),
    Maureen Bynes (Mrs. Warren), Britt Leach (Parson Weems),
    Anne Ramsey (Spinster), Don McGovern (Norvell), Dennis Fimple
    (Hangman), Nancy Coan Kaclik (Miriam), Lin Shaye (Parasol Lady),
    R. L. Armstrong (Farmer)
Released: October 6, 1978
Specs: 109 minutes; Metrocolor
Availability: DVD (Paramount)

Although Mike Nichols's *The Fortune* was a disappointment as a film, it did allow Nicholson to explore doing comedy. This was one of the elements that helped his second directorial effort, *Goin' South*. Nicholson draws from past roles and the influence of past directors to make a film that was a critical and box office failure in its time, but has since increased a bit in popularity.

Nicholson plays Henry Moon, a small-time western outlaw whose manic behavior and general ineptitude are exhibited in the opening scene, where he is chased by lawmen. After riding through a river, he gets off of his horse and starts triumphantly dancing to celebrate that he is now in Mexico and therefore out of their jurisdiction. He is wrong, and the lawmen continue after him, just as his horse drops into a dead faint. He is lassoed, taken to jail, and set to be hanged.

When Nicholson dances about and merrily shouts that he is safely in Mexico, it is not unlike the passionate outburst of McMurphy in *One Flew over the Cuckoo's Nest*. Moon is as unstable as McMurphy, and also as thoughtful, with the same inability to maintain some semblance of structure and control.

The character's response to straight-faced women who come in to stare at him in jail is a combination of confusion and anger. He is not told that these women are examining him as a possible matrimonial prospect, as the law in this area states that a man who does not commit murder can be saved from the hangman's noose by a woman willing to marry him. When this is finally revealed to him as he walks toward the gallows, he makes impassioned pleas for one of the women he insulted to spare his life. Finally, an older woman agrees. He comes down and embraces her, and she drops dead.

The boisterous humor, some of it a bit dark, makes for an effective opening. Nicholson, as director, uses expansive long shots in the outdoor scenes, and tight close-ups for the characters, obviously inspired by Monte Hellman, who'd directed some of his previous films in a western setting. However, this promising opening doesn't maintain the same rhythm or attitude once the story is introduced. Julia Tate, an attractive, virginal woman, spares Moon's life by agreeing to marry him, and the movie then focuses on their off-kilter relationship. She uses him to work on her gold mine, with no intention of a sexual relationship, reminding him that his only other choice is the gallows. Skeptical that there is any gold in the mine, Moon asks for some gloves to avoid blisters on his hands. Julia states, "Blisters on the hands is better than rope burns on the neck." Moon has no choice but to agree to her demands.

In one scene, Moon succumbs to an explosion of sexual frustration, ties Julia to their bed, and that is how they consummate the marriage. Oddly, Julia thereafter warms up to Moon's oddball behavior, his bulging eyes, and crooked brow. However, when they discover gold in her mine, Julia indicates that the gold is hers, treating Moon like a mere worker rather than a husband or partner. However, she eventually agrees to give him 50 percent of the gold, believing it's the right thing to do. She apologizes for being "greedy and selfish." Despite her becoming more comfortable with Moon, Julia still admonishes him for "acting foolish." Moon responds to her stuffiness with, "I wish you'd try it some time."

There are several tangential conflicts that occur within the parameters of the film's narrative structure. The deputy hates Moon because he considers Julia his girl (although this is never indicated with any real evidence). Moon's old outlaw gang tries to get involved when they discover that he and Julia are mining for gold. Moon considers stealing the gold from Julia.

Mary Steenburgen, making her film debut, is effective in the role of Julia, which had been turned down by Jane Fonda, Jessica Lange, and Meryl Streep. Steenburgen was discovered in the casting office by Nicholson, who read the part with her and took a chance on casting the newcomer in the role. Nicholson also found room for actor friends like Christopher Lloyd and Danny DeVito, both of whom appeared with him in *One Flew over the Cuckoo's Nest*.

John Belushi, by then quite popular on TV's *Saturday Night Live*, also made his film debut in *Goin' South*, although it was released after his second film, *National Lampoon's Animal House* (1978). According to Patrick McGilligan in the biography *Jack's Life*,

> Belushi was one jarring note in the proceedings. On the one hand, Jack wanted to like the comedian, whose popularity was soaring. Belushi blustered and posed, but he was fundamentally sweet, the kind of guy Nicholson liked to take under his wing. . . . However, Belushi had a short fuse. He made petty demands and fought with the *Goin' South* producers, especially Harold Schneider, whose job it was not to lose fights. The television comedian became progressively more sulky as filming dragged on and, partly in response to his behavior, his role seemed to shrink.[1]

After the film, Belushi had harsh words for the experience, stating, "Jack treated me like shit on *Goin' South*. I hate him. If I see him, I'll punch him."[2]

Nicholson shot *Goin' South* in Durango, Mexico, where many John Wayne westerns had been filmed. Its locations were many of the same used in Wayne's 1970 film *Chisum*. His sequence of shots, his framing of the action, and his use of the background imagery to frame the outdoor scenes are all visually effective. Nicholson stated that his intention was to make a comedy in the same manner as Preston Sturges or Ernst Lubitsch used to make. However, *Goin' South* is a disjointed aesthetic failure, sustained only by Nicholson's bravura acting and Mary Steenburgen's effective debut performance. Among the negative reviews was this one from *Variety*, which stated,

> Jack Nicholson playing Gabby Hayes is interesting, even amusing at times, but Hayes was never a leading man, which *Goin' South* desperately needs. Picture starts off promisingly enough with Nicholson as a hapless outlaw who makes it across the border but the posse cheats and comes across after him causing his horse to faint. On his way to the gallows, Nicholson discovers an unordinary county ordinance that would allow him to go free if picked for marriage by a maiden lady in town. Up to now, *Goin' South* is still going strong. But here it stops as lovely young Mary Steenburgen steps out of the crowd and agrees to marry the bearded, dirty horse-thief. Why she should do this is never satisfactorily established in the script carrying the names of four writers. Ostensibly, it's to get the manpower to help her mine her property for gold before the railroad takes over. But it never jells, as Nicholson continues to sputter and chomp, acting more like her grandfather than a handsome roué out to overcome her virginity.[3]

Still, *Goin' South* is significant among Nicholson's films because of its off-beat nature, his approach to directing, his delineation of the character, and its pivotal place in the transition from *One Flew over the Cuckoo's Nest* to *The Shining*. Each of these films allows the actor to explore different types of oddball characters and from a different perspective. For *One Flew over the Cuckoo's Nest*, it was for drama. For *Goin' South*, it was for comedy. And for his next film, Stanley Kubrick's *The Shining*, based on the Stephen King novel, it was for horror.

THE SHINING

(1980, Warner Bros.)

★ ★ ★ ★ ★

Director: Stanley Kubrick
Screenplay: Stanley Kubrick, Diane Johnson, based on the novel by Stephen
    King
Producer: Stanley Kubrick. *Cinematographer:* John Alcott. *Editor:* Ray Lovejoy
Cast: Jack Nicholson (Jack Torrance), Shelley Duvall (Wendy Torrance),
    Danny Lloyd (Danny Torrance), Scatman Crothers (Dick Hallorann),
    Barry Nelson (Stuart Ullman), Philip Stone (Delbert Grady), Joe
    Turkel (Lloyd the Bartender), Anne Jackson (Doctor), Tony Burton
    (Larry Durkin), Lia Beldam (Young Woman in Bath), Billie Gibson (Old
    Woman in Bath), Barry Dennen (Bill Watson), Lisa and Louise Burns
    (Grady Daughters), Alison Coleridge (Secretary), Burnell Tucker
    (Policeman), Jana Shelden (Stewardess), Kate Phelps (Receptionist),
    Norman Gay (Injured Guest), Vivian Kubrick (Guest on Couch in
    Ballroom), Bertha Lynn (Newscaster), Derek Lyons (Bellhop), Glenn
    Rinker (Himself)
Released: May 23, 1980
Specs: 146 minutes[1]; color
Availability: DVD (Warner)

The Shining is a film that received lackluster reviews upon its initial release and soon grew in its reputation as one of the finest horror films in cinema's rich history. Much of the credit will invariably go to Stanley Kubrick, but the performances by the entire cast, especially Jack Nicholson and Shelley Duvall, are just as important to the film's aesthetic success. Once again Nicholson draws from elements of past characters to play a recovering alcoholic who descends more and more deeply into madness. The quiet cool of J. J. Gittes, the manic outburst of McMurphy, even the jittery confusion of Rexford Bedlo in *The Raven* are among the ingredients that help to compile the myriad of personality traits in Jack Torrance.

By the time he made *The Shining*, Stanley Kubrick had already emerged as one of cinema's finest directors, having helmed such films as *Paths of Glory* (1959), *Spartacus* (1962), *Dr. Strangelove or How I Learned to Stop Worrying and Love the Bomb* (1964), *2001: A Space Odyssey* (1968), and *A Clockwork Orange* (1971). Kubrick investigated different genres in his directorial career, always exploring the edgier elements of each. Horror seemed like a natural area for him to explore; in fact, he had been offered the chance to direct *The Exorcist* (1973) years earlier, but he turned it down, as he wanted to also be the film's producer. *The Shining* is Kubrick's attempt to make what he called "the world's scariest movie."[2] He enlisted the help of Diane Johnson, due to admiring her book *The Shadow Knows*, and the two worked on the screenplay for eleven weeks.

Jack Torrance has left his teaching career to be a writer. He takes a job as a caretaker in an out-of-the-way Colorado hotel that is not in operation for several months a year due to heavy snow. The owner who interviews Jack explains that he will be cooped up alone in the massive building with his wife and child, and this seclusion caused a former caretaker to crack and kill his family. Torrance states that the seclusion will be perfect for him to work on his writing.

Jack's wife, Wendy, and young son, Danny, have their own issues. Danny sees visions, has an imaginary friend, and is in the care of a therapist who visits the home. Wendy mindlessly accepts situations without any concentration. She is matter-of-fact about Danny's visions and exhibits the same lack of concern when she indicates to the therapist that Jack once dislocated their son's shoulder by pulling his arm too forcefully. Once the family is at the hotel, Danny discovers that the cook has the same telepathic powers that cause visions. They communicate telepathically and later privately discuss their shared powers. The cook refers to it as "shining." He tells Danny that room 237 of the hotel has a shine of its own and warns him to never enter it.

It is from this premise that the film then becomes a character study where each of the individuals evolves. Jack slowly descends into madness buoyed not only by the isolation but also his lack of writing success. Danny's visions become more intense, and the child's behavior becomes more withdrawn and distant. Wendy's aloof acceptance evolves into panic as things become stranger and more unsettling.

Director Kubrick creates a perfect atmosphere of isolation using overhead establishing shots to show how the hotel is framed by tall trees, the winding road looking small and narrow in this visual context. Whenever anyone is outside, he surrounds them with negative space, the figures seeming small when surrounded by the vastness of the area. Indoors, Kubrick follows the actors with a series of tracking shots, using deep focus to show the depth of each room. They are always off-kilter, even in the earlier scenes in which Jack is first being interviewed for his position. As Jack is being pleasantly informed of his duties and given background on the hotel, there is a shot of another man, who sits and does not speak. It is only seconds long, before it cuts back to Jack's interview. When the cook and Danny sit at a table discussing their telepathic similarities, Kubrick moves in closer, with no negative space, cutting between the two actors, forcing the viewer's attention.

Kubrick's framework remains effective once the characters become the focus of the narrative. Danny's visions are filled with frightening imagery containing murdered twin girls and cascades of bloody pools filling the halls. Jack's initial edginess reaches violent outbursts and visions of his own. He is found yelling in his sleep in front of his typewriter. When awakened, he says he had a nightmare that he murdered Wendy and Danny. Wendy finds a bruise on Danny and accuses Jack of hurting him. Jack goes into the ballroom and pours his heart out to a ghostly bartender. When Danny claims a woman in room 237 tried to strangle him, Jack investigates and sees a beautiful naked woman. When Jack kisses her, she turns into a rotting dead corpse. He tells his wife he saw nothing in the room. Jack then attends a ghost-filled 1920s party in the ballroom, where he reconnects with the bartender, who seems to understand him. He also meets the former caretaker who killed his family (including the young girls Danny sees) and now instructs Jack to "correct" his wife and child. It is the surreal elements and ghosts that inhabit *The Shining* that place it more comfortably in the horror genre than, say, suspense.

At this point Jack completely snaps and terrorizes Wendy, whose own emotional collapse is really the axis of the film's narrative. She can't reach Danny, she can't escape Jack, and the changes, without explanation, are

Jack Torrance encounters one of several apparitions in *The Shining*, with Joe Turkel as the bartender. *Warner Bros. / Photofest © Warner Bros.*

forcing her into a full emotional panic. And, still, she is the center of the story, the anchored character who is responding to the others but remaining normal and focused. Kubrick beautifully shoots the more terrorizing scenes between Jack and Wendy, editing from shots of Wendy facing Jack, and of Jack facing Wendy, as he slowly goes after her on a staircase and she fends him off with a baseball bat. She hits him hard enough to daze him, he falls down the stairs, and she locks him away in a store room. The shot of Wendy's skinny frame dragging Jack is from the floor, from his perspective. He is not unconscious. He is only dazed. Once he is locked in, Jack pounds and says, "Let me out and I'll forget the whole goddamn thing as if nothing ever happened," and "I think you hurt my head real bad. I need a doctor." Kubrick continues to shoot Nicholson from the floor, pointing the camera upward toward his face, his hair unkempt and falling, framing his facial expression and adding to the creepy imagery.

Jack is visited by the former caretaker's ghost again, who frees him from isolation. Danny keeps muttering and writing "Redrum," indicating to Wendy that Danny's imaginary friend has completely overtaken his personality. Then, in one of the most iconic moments in *The Shining*, Jack bursts through a door with an ax, sticks his head through the opening, and yells, "Here's Johnny!" Now that we are into the twenty-first century, it is likely that some viewers will not understand the allusion to what was then a popular catchphrase. The NBC program *The Tonight Show* was, at that time, hosted by Johnny Carson. His announcer, Ed McMahon, would open each show by saying, "Here's Johnny." Nicholson reportedly ad-libbed the line, and Kubrick almost used another take without it. Fortunately, he changed his mind.[3]

One of the most impressively shot sequences in the film is when the cook returns to the hotel to investigate, his powers informing him that there is danger. Kubrick shoots actor Scatman Crothers walking toward the camera from a long hallway, tracking his movements as he comes closer to the frame. Once he has reached that point, Kubrick switches shots, filming him from behind, as he continues to slowly walk and call out "Anybody here?" The tension of his slow movement along with Kubrick's tracking shot is disrupted by the sudden appearance of Jack, who murders the cook with an ax.

The film concludes after Wendy and Danny escape Jack by running through an outdoor maze, finding the snowcat vehicle that the cook used to return to the hotel through the snowy mountain roads, and leaving Jack to freeze to death. Kubrick shoots this with almost no light, the color blue permeating the visual. A final daylight shot of a frozen, dead Jack Torrance ends the scene. The final tracking shot closes in on a 1921 ballroom photo in which Jack appears, which is the last thing we see.

There are several elements to *The Shining* that add nuance to each scene. Kubrick carefully instructed the extras during the ballroom scene to behave naturally and not engage in florid gestures, enhancing the scene's realism. The people are essentially just part of the background to frame Nicholson in the foreground as he enters. The tracking shot of Danny riding his Big Wheel bike through the hotel's cavernous hallways was accomplished with a special low-pole version of the Steadicam developed for this film. One scene, when Wendy sees that all Jack has been typing is "All work and no play make Jack a dull boy," was shot several times, from several angles, showing the typewritten pages in different languages, sometimes not translating too closely to the English phrase. For the typewriter sound effect in an earlier scene where we see Jack typing, Kubrick recorded someone actually typing out the phrase "All work and no play make Jack a dull boy" because he had heard that some keys on a typewriter make different sounds—more evidence regarding the amount of effort and thought he put into each scene.

Filming *The Shining* was very difficult for the actors. Kubrick would frequently add to or change the script, to the point where Nicholson was frequently tossing aside new pages of the script, tired of repeatedly relearning his part due to the constant changes being made. It reached the point where Nicholson was learning his lines only minutes before filming them.

Kubrick was also a perfectionist and, like Charlie Chaplin, was known for doing multiple takes on a single scene, sometimes as many as forty. Nicholson found this to be so tedious that when he returned to the set in January after a break for Christmas, his interest in the project had waned. A fire on the set further delayed production. However, despite Nicholson's personal feelings while making the project, his performance level never wavers.

The Shining shows Nicholson at peak madness. We knew based on his previous performances that he could play crazy characters, but this is his first film in which his character's craziness is designed to frighten the viewer. The scariest scenes aren't the ones where he's yelling and carrying on, like the "Here's Johnny" bit (which comes off as darkly amusing), but when he's acting relatively calm. One of the most chilling scenes is when he confronts Wendy on the staircase and calmly tells her, "I'm not gonna hurt you. I'm just going to bash your brains in."

Despite what is now considered a brilliant performance, alongside some of Nicholson's best, the author of the original book was not impressed. Stephen King told *Playboy* in 1983,

> Jack Nicholson, though a fine actor, was all wrong for the part. His last big role had been in *One Flew over the Cuckoo's Nest*, and between that and the manic grin, the audience automatically identified him as a loony from the first scene. But the book is about Jack Torrance's gradual descent into madness through the malign influence of the Overlook—if the guy is nuts to begin with, then the entire tragedy of his downfall is wasted.[4]

A revealing "Making Of" documentary shows how Jack Nicholson prepared for the scene where he is chopping through the door with an ax. He goes from kibitzing with Kubrick's daughter Vivian, who is behind the camera, to getting into character so he can let go of inhibition. It also shows the cameraman lying on the floor shooting upward at Nicholson in the scene where he is locked in the store room. We see him leaving his mad character and returning to the rather pleasant actor who kibitzes in a friendly manner with the crew and visitors to the set.

Nicholson believed Shelley Duvall had the most difficult role in the project and was impressed with how well she rose to the occasion. Duvall told Roger Ebert in a 1980 interview,

Jack Nicholson's character had to be crazy and angry all the time. And my character had to cry 12 hours a day, all day long, the last nine months straight, five or six days a week. After I all that work, hardly anyone even criticized my performance, even to mention. . . . The reviews were all about Kubrick, like I wasn't there.[5]

Shelley Duvall became so ill from the stress of her role and her difficulty getting along with Kubrick that her hair started to fall out. She stated in the "Making Of" documentary,

From May until October I was really in and out of ill health, because the stress of the role was so great, and I just got out of a relationship. So to me it was just tumultuous.

The documentary shows her pulling strands of hair off of her head that are falling out, even pointing this out to Kubrick.

Danny Lloyd, who memorably played Danny Torrance, was only five years old, and Kubrick was very protective of the child on the set so he would not be frightened. Lloyd made no other movies. He was interviewed at age forty by the *New York Daily News* in 2013[6] and recalled that he tried out for parts for years after that but never got any. He finally gave up and "went back to being a regular kid." He did not even see the film until he was sixteen, and his fondest memories were riding his bike on the set and playing with the Burns girls, who appeared as the twins.

In her *New York Times* review, Janet Maslin recognized the importance of the film's performances:

Mr. Nicholson's Jack is one of his most vibrant characterizations, furiously alive in every frame and fueled by an explosive anger. Mr. Nicholson is also devilishly funny, from his sarcastic edge at the film's beginning to his cry of "Heeere's Johnny!" as he chops down a bathroom door to get to Miss Duvall. Though Miss Duvall's Wendy at first seems a strange match for Mr. Nicholson, she eventually takes shape as an almost freakish cipher, her early banality making her terror all the more extreme. Danny Lloyd, as Danny, and Scatman Crothers, as the hotel chef who, like Danny, has psychic powers, both give keen, steady performances as the story's relatively naturalistic figures. Barry Nelson is a model of false assurance as the hotel manager.[7]

The Shining is so layered and so ambiguous, it is still being analyzed in the twenty-first century. There have been countless theories regarding the film's themes, involving everything from the doubles seen throughout the film, to the ghosts, to even the Holocaust. It's also a movie that, for some viewers, needs time to sink in. There are aspects of it that can be confusing, but it was never meant to be a straightforward story, and there's usually something new to discover upon repeated viewings.

The Shining works on every level, emerging as yet another one of the timeless classics in which Jack Nicholson stars and turns in a truly remarkable performance. It is also one of a great director's finest films, contains some of the best work from actors Shelley Duvall and Scatman Crothers, and is dotted with special moments from the players of small parts, such as Phillip Stone as the evil former caretaker and Joe Turkel as the ghostly bartender. Turkel had appeared in two previous Kubrick films (*The Killing* [1956] and *Paths of Glory* [1957]).

Following his work in *The Shining*, Nicholson next appeared opposite Jessica Lange in a steamy remake of the 1946 Tay Garnett film *The Postman Always Rings Twice*, which featured John Garfield and Lana Turner. Based on James M. Cain's novel, the 1981 remake was directed by Nicholson's old friend Bob Rafelson and received a very poor reaction from critics and audiences. One of the chief problems was that the later film did not explain the significance of the title, and the ending of the remake was much weaker. *The Postman Always Rings Twice* was a movie that did not need to be remade. It does have some significance as being the first erotic thriller of the era, followed by such films as *Body Heat* (1981), *Fatal Attraction* (1987), and *Basic Instinct* (1992). Jack Nicholson then went into Warren Beatty's film *Reds*, in which he was cast as playwright Eugene O'Neill. Even though it was only a supporting role and this would clearly be Warren Beatty's film from his vision, Nicholson felt comfortable being able to explore a real-life character in a project that seemed quite promising.

REDS

(1981, Paramount)

★ ★ ★ ½

Director: Warren Beatty
Screenplay: Warren Beatty, Trevor Griffiths, based on the book by John Reed
Producers: Warren Beatty, David L. MacLeod, Simon Relph, Dede Allen.
    Cinematographer: Vittorio Storaro. *Editors:* Dede Allen, Craig McKay
Cast: Warren Beatty (John Reed), Diane Keaton (Louise Bryant), Edward
    Herrmann (Max Eastman), Jerzy Kosinski (Grigory Zinoviev), Jack
    Nicholson (Eugene O'Neill), Paul Sorvino (Louis Fraina), Maureen
    Stapleton (Emma Goldman), Nicolas Coster (Paul Trullinger), M.
    Emmet Walsh (Speaker at Liberal Club), Bessie Love (Mrs. Partlow),
    Ian Wolfe (Mr. Partlow), George Plimpton (Horace Whigham), Dolph
    Sweet (Big Bill Haywood), Max Weight (Floyd Deli), MacIntyre Dixon
    (Carl Walters), Pat Starr (Helen Walters), Eleanor D. Wilson (Mrs.
    Reed), Gene Hackman (Pete Van Wherry), Gerald Hiken (Dr. Lorber),
    William Daniels (Julius Gerber), Dave King (Allan Benson), Josephy
    Buloff (Joe Volski), Stefan Gryff (Alex Gomberg), Roger Sloman
    (Lenin), Shane Rimmer (MacAlpine), Jerry Hardin (Harry),
    R. G. Armstrong (Agent), Josef Sommer (State Department Official),
    Andreas La Casa (Boy), Roger Baldwin, Henry Miller, Adele Rogers
    St. Johns, Dora Russell, Scott Nearing, Tess Davis, Heaton Vorse,
    Hamilton Fish, Isaac Don Levine, Rebecca West, Will Durant, Will
    Weinstone, Emmanuel Herbert, Arne Swabeck, Adele Gutman
    Nathan, George Seldes, Kenneth Chamberlain, Blanche Hays Fagen,
    Galina Von Meck, Art Shields, Andrew Dasburg, Hugo Geller,

Dorothy Frooks, George Jessel, Jack Bailin, Lucita Williams, Bernadie
Szold-Fritz, Jessica Smith, Harry Carlisle, Arthur Mayer (Themselves)
Released: December 25, 1981
Specs: 194 minutes; color
Availability: DVD (Paramount)

Using filmed witness accounts interspersed with narrative cinema, pro-
ducer-writer-director Warren Beatty examines the life and exploits of John
Reed, while also starring as Reed. It is an enormous task to maintain all of
these areas in an epic film that exceeds a three-hour running time.

John Reed was born to privilege in 1887, educated at Harvard, and
displayed all the traits of refinement as he pursued a journalism career.
He became a leftist while reporting from Russia as the Bolsheviks rose to
power. He published the book *Ten Days That Shook the World* in 1919.
He died a year later, as a member of the Soviet propaganda ministry, and
is the only American buried in the Kremlin. Warren Beatty was intrigued
by Reed's story and began exploring the possibility of filming it as early as
1966. Several witnesses who knew Reed were interviewed, some as early as
1971. Notables such as Roger Nash Baldwin, the founder of the American
Civil Liberties Union; comedian George Jessel; novelist Henry Miller; and
journalist Adela Rogers St. Johns were among those interviewed. Beatty
wrote a script with Trevor Griffiths that was completed in 1976. It went
through several writer contributions, including Robert Towne and Elaine
May, before Beatty finally deemed it ready to be filmed. In a retrospective
article, *Vanity Fair* stated,

> Not only did *Reds* pioneer the blend of fact and fiction that later came to be
> known as "docudrama," it was also an unapologetic, if critical, major-studio
> treatment of Communism, lavishing on this mostly taboo subject the vast
> resources at Hollywood's disposal: a big budget, A-list stars, and, in this case,
> the brains, skills, and talents of the best and the brightest of Hollywood's most
> recent—and probably final—golden age. All of this at a moment that could
> not have been less hospitable to the subject. Beatty began shooting the picture
> in 1979, the year the Russians invaded Afghanistan; production continued
> throughout 1980, the year America elected a new president, Ronald Reagan,
> who campaigned with open hostility to the Soviet Union and, once in office,
> would famously dub it the "evil empire." *Reds* was so unlikely a film for Hol-

lywood, and its timing so unpropitious, that many in Beatty's orbit, including the screenwriter Robert Towne and the film critic Pauline Kael, begged him not to make it, convinced that *Reds* was a folly.[1]

Reds is a sweeping epic that has two parts. The first deals with Reed meeting Louise Bryant in 1915 and their tumultuous relationship. Like Reed, Bryant is borne of privilege but attracted by radical leftist idealism. She escapes from her societal surroundings via her own writing. The second part of the film deals with the last year of Reed's life, after the publication of *Ten Days That Shook the World*.

In a book about Jack Nicholson, we must concentrate on the O'Neill role. This comes to life especially in 1916 when Reed is in St. Louis covering the Democratic National Convention. Bryant develops a relationship with O'Neill, continues her feminist manifestos, and gets more involved with a group of leftist artists, musicians, actors, and activists. Nicholson plays the role of O'Neill in a very subdued, controlled manner. He is quiet, taut, and effectively charismatic. He is very measured in comparison to Beatty's more enthusiastic Reed character. These traits are nicely presented when Reed returns home and sees, from a distance, Bryant and O'Neill stand-

Nicholson as playwright Eugene O'Neill, Diane Keaton as Louise Bryant, and Warren Beatty as John Reed in *Reds*. *Paramount Pictures / Photofest © Paramount Pictures*

ing closely and gazing at each other romantically. They do not realize he has returned home. When he enters, during a party, he is welcomed by all except O'Neill, whose unhappiness at Reed's return is obvious by his expression. Reed is asked to tell of his exploits while away. He does so rapidly, nervously, exhibiting his tension while O'Neill continues to bottle his up. Later that night, Reed proposes to Bryant, realizing that may be the only way to keep her.

O'Neill hovers about as Bryant packs to move. He asks for a drink and gives her a poem he's written proclaiming his love for her. He says, "You can sleep with whoever you want, live with whoever you want, I'll do whatever you say. I'd like to kill you, but I can't. So you can do whatever you want, except not see me." It is then that Bryant reveals that she and Reed have married. He continues, "Does this mean we have to cheat, or is this a free and independent marriage?" His tone then becomes accusatory: "You used me to get Jack Reed to marry you!" Once he leaves, she gently places the poem in a book. O'Neill comes up again when Reed finds the poem in the book several months later. Reed is unhappy but forgiving as he admits to his own infidelities just as long ago.

Nicholson's control, his maintaining a quiet demeanor that still exhibits great tension, completely dominates this scene. It also offers further evidence of his versatility as an actor. After the more manic characters in *One Flew over the Cuckoo's Nest* and *The Shining*, Nicholson's take on O'Neill is even more low key than his J. J. Gittes in *Chinatown*. O'Neill confesses he is "crazy about" Bryant, alternating between seething anger and enormous hurt. But his voice barely rises above a whisper as he leaves and says, "I wish you well. You and Jack." Nicholson realizes O'Neill is as privileged as either Reed or Bryant, but his activism does not venture past the written word. He is smarter, more articulate, but just as emotionally vulnerable. The bitter front he puts on barely masks how devastated he is at losing Bryant to Reed.

Overall, *Reds* is at times compelling, but occasionally rather dull. As with many epics this large, the film is often bloated and less interesting. Beatty is quite impressive when one considers the multitasking necessary to maintain his many roles in the production (he originally wanted John Lithgow for the role of Reed, as Lithgow resembles him). Warren Beatty became the third person to be nominated for Academy Awards in the three categories of Best Actor, Best Director, and Best Original Screenplay in a film that was also nominated for the Best Picture Oscar. The others were Woody Allen for *Annie Hall* (1977), in which Diane Keaton played the title role, and Orson

Welles for *Citizen Kane* (1941). It was nominated in the four major acting categories—the last film to achieve this until *Silver Linings Playbook* over thirty years later.

The production was quite grueling, running nearly a year and well over its intended budget. Beatty and Keaton were a couple off screen, but the difficulties in filming *Reds* were said to have ended their relationship. Beatty also had a conflict with cinematographer Vittorio Storaro, who wanted more fluid shots, while Beatty preferred static ones. Beatty insisted on many takes, even when working with seasoned actors like Paul Sorvino and Gene Hackman. The scene where Reed is told that his wife has lost her job took an alleged 100 takes, and only because Hackman refused to do 101. *Vanity Fair* published the following interview with Hackman:

> "It was such a pleasure to work for Warren, even though he did a lot of takes," the actor says. "It was close to 50. He didn't say a lot to me. There's something about somebody who is that tough and perseveres that way that is attractive to an actor that wants to do good work. So I hung in there. And finally it gets you out of the text. You just have these words that are flowing out of you. But all those takes—I was going blind. After Take 5, I'm kind of finished. I had no idea how they would change. I don't think that I ever verbalized anything to him in terms of my annoyance—I just sucked it up—but he must have known. When he called me to do *Dick Tracy*"—the film Beatty made for Disney, in 1990—"I said, 'I love you, Warren, but I just can't do it.'"[2]

Reds has some problems, but it is overall quite an impressive film, and one of the better examples of that period's epic cinema that also includes *Heaven's Gate* and *Apocalypse Now*. It is essential to Jack Nicholson's filmography, not only for his Oscar nomination, but also because the scenes in which he appears are perhaps the best in the entire 194-minute production. In a comparatively small, supporting role, Jack Nicholson effectively steals the film from the formidable cast.

Upon completing his work on *Reds*, Nicholson starred as a border patrol agent in *The Border* (1982). It is not one of the actor's better films, casting him as a hardworking man who decides to break the law in order to gain more money and offer his demanding wife a more affluent lifestyle. Nicholson wavers between the personality of a man who is content with simply providing for his family and his need to take chances by smuggling immigrants across the border in order to have enough of an income to please his wife. His role then extends to altruism when a young woman's baby is abducted with the intent of putting it up for sale, and he tries to help her.

Nicholson's previous few films had been nominated for many Oscars, even if they did not always resonate at the box office. *The Border* received no Oscar interest and was also a box office disappointment. This was merely an aberration, however, as Nicholson's following film returned him to a much loftier level aesthetically and financially.

TERMS OF ENDEARMENT

(1983, Paramount)

★ ★ ★ ★ ★

Director: James L. Brooks
Screenplay: James L. Brooks, Larry McMurtry
Producer: James L. Brooks. *Cinematographer:* Andrzej Bartkowiak. *Editors:*
    Richard Marks, Sidney Wolinsky
Cast: Debra Winger (Emma Greenway), Shirley MacLaine (Aurora
    Greenway), Jack Nicholson (Garrett Breedlove), Jeff Daniels (Flap),
    John Lithgow (Sam), Danny DeVito (Vernon Dahlart), Lisa Hart
    Carroll (Patsy), Betty R. King (Rosie), Huckleberry Fox (Teddy),
    Troy Bishop (Tommy), Megan Morris (Melanie), Norman Bennett
    (Edward Johnson), Kate Charleson (Janice), Tom Wees (Dr. Budge),
    Paul Menzel (Dr. Maise), Amanda Watkins (Meg), Buddy Gilbert (Dr.
    Ratcher), David Wohl (Phil), Leslie Folse (Doris), Sharisse Baker (Lee
    Anne), Devon O'Brien (Lizbeth), Tara Yeakey (Melanie as a Baby),
    Jennifer Josey (Young Emma), Shane Sherwin (Young Tommy), Sandra
    Newkirk (Mrs. Johnson), Mary Kay Place (Voice)
Released: December 9, 1983
Specs: 132 minutes; Metrocolor
Availability: DVD (Paramount)

Despite his having achieved awards, nominations, and superstardom for starring roles in great films, by 1982 Jack Nicholson was content in taking a supporting role in *Terms of Endearment*. Based on the novel by Larry McMurtry, who'd also penned *The Last Picture Show* and *Lonesome Dove*, this is the story of a quirky mother and daughter trying to makes sense of life's ceaseless changes. However, in a book about Jack Nicholson's films, our concentration is on his supporting role as former astronaut Garrett Breedlove, who lives next door. Garrett is a cynical, hard-drinking womanizer whose inherent charisma attracts the mother, Aurora, from afar.

Aurora is dealing with being alone after her daughter, Emma, moves away with her new husband, of whom Aurora does not approve. The dynamic between the two women is fraught with tension and examined over a period of years. While their love for each other is undeniable, Aurora is more withdrawn, while Emma is impulsive. Emma marries shortly after graduating from high school and goes away with Flap, her husband, when he gets a job in Iowa. Years go by, and the marriage weakens due to Flap's unfaithfulness. By the time Emma is pregnant with a third child, her money is so low she has to call Aurora and ask for financial help. The well-to-do Aurora tries to talk her into having an abortion. Emma has the baby, as well as an affair with Sam Burns, a banker who is a few years older.

Emma's life is somehow grounded due to the children, but her marriage is confronted by several challenges. Most of the reason why she doesn't leave Flap is to avoid giving Aurora the satisfaction of being proved right, although Emma does move back in with her mother, along with her children, upon first discovering Flap's affair with a student. The trajectory of the narrative changes when Emma discovers during a routine checkup that she has lymphoma, and everyone around her becomes concerned. When the initial treatment is without success, they all realize the inevitable.

Nicholson's role is comparatively small, but it remains significant throughout. His scenes with MacLaine are the best scenes. His dialogue is the strongest and sharpest. And his character is the most complex. While the lonely Aurora has been attracted to him from afar, Garrett does not appear to realize her existence at all. Finally, he confronts her and starts a conversation. This results in a lunch date, sex, and a level of carefree fun that Aurora appears to have heretofore never experienced. When they are having lunch together, they engage in the following dialogue:

Aurora: That's very rude, looking at another woman while you're out to lunch with me.

Garrett: What we need to do is get drunk.

Shirley MacLaine, Debra Winger, and Nicholson in *Terms of Endearment. Paramount Pictures / Photofest © Paramount Pictures*

Aurora: I do not get drunk, and I do not approve of escorts who get drunk.

Garrett: Well I've made a study of this situation and I've arrived at certain conclusions, and I think that what *you* need is a *lot* of drinks.

This is followed with the reckless abandon of Garrett sitting atop the front seat of his convertible and maneuvering the steering wheel with his feet while Aurora has her foot on the gas pedal. Garrett, the astronaut, has endured pressure. He has seen men die. Nicholson told Roger Ebert in an interview, "One of the things I learned while I was reading *The Right Stuff* was that 40 percent of the graduating classes of those guys died."[1] Thus, the uninhibited feeling Garrett enjoys with Aurora is a release, an escape from whatever made him the drunken cynic he has become. For Aurora it is a different kind of release—from her widowhood, her celibacy, the distance from her daughter, and her disapproval of her daughter's marriage.

However, Garrett and Aurora's tenuous relationship is strained when the bachelor has to deal with Emma and her children moving back in with Aurora. He breaks up with Aurora, but returns once Emma's illness becomes serious. "Who would ever have guessed you'd turn out to be a nice guy,"

Aurora says to him. She also admits, as he is leaving, that she loves him. When she gets no response as he leaves, she calls him back over and demands one. "I almost made a clean getaway," he says. Then, finally, "I love you too, kid." Once again Nicholson's natural charm and charisma oozes through the character he is playing. Garrett is the classic cynic, unable to, and uninterested in, putting up with the behaviors of others that offer him even the most marginal inconvenience.

Most of the film centers upon Aurora and Emma's relationship, extending to Flap and the children. The oldest boy resents the fact that his mother is terminally ill and reacts in anger in order to deal with his sorrow. Aurora wants to adopt the youngest child, a daughter, but neither Flap nor Emma want the family to break up. Emma confronts her oldest child by stating, "I know that you love me." During an emotional confrontation when the boy speaks negatively about his mother, he is slapped by Aurora, and he ends up weeping in his grandmother's arms. Emma dies later that night. The film concludes with Garrett showing up at Emma's wake, and immediately connecting with the children, especially the oldest boy. Whatever misgivings this never-married former astronaut once had about the children, he shows he has overcome them due to his love for Aurora. Jack Nicholson told Roger Ebert in an interview,

> Breedlove may have a lot of things screwy with him. He may be claustrophobic, he may be squeamish about diseases, but when the actual problem of bereavement presents itself, he's your man. He can handle it.[2]

Aurora and Emma are masterfully played by Shirley MacLaine and Debra Winger, but the actresses reportedly did not get along due to their very different methods of preparing for a scene. Allegedly they even got into a shoving match during filming. However, specific scenes are very impressive, such as Aurora screaming at the nurse's station in the hospital for one of them to give Emma something for her pain, or Emma trying to make sense of her situation while visiting a wealthy friend in New York whose circle is filled with working women who are self-centered and condescending.

Despite his small role, Jack Nicholson steals every scene in which he appears. His character of Garrett was created for the movie by screenwriter James Brooks specifically for Burt Reynolds. Because he was contractually committed to *The Cannonball Run*, Reynolds had to turn the project down. Paul Newman also passed before the role was given to Nicholson. Reynolds would later state on TV's *Larry King Live*, "There are no awards in Hollywood for being an idiot."[3]

At the time he made *Terms of Endearment*, Nicholson had been off screen for nearly two years. His previous film, *The Border*, was released in February 1982, and this film was not in wide release until toward the end of 1983. Nicholson told *Rolling Stone* in an interview,

> I had a wonderful summer with one of my favorite people, who passed on this year, Sam Spiegel. In that two years I think I spent one whole summer with Sam, just like his sidekick. He was certainly an inspiration; those movies he made in the Fifties were the movies, just about. Sam's lesson to me was always to go for quality. This is not where producers are at anymore. Everyone said, "Oh, God, you won't be able not to work for six months—you'll be a dead man." Well, I never missed it. And when I came back to work, great; I talked to Jim Brooks, made the deal with him over the telephone.[4]

Brooks had been a TV director, helming episodes of *M*A*S*H* and *The Mary Tyler Moore Show*, among others. This was his first feature film. Nicholson had to confess to Brooks that because he never watched television, he had not seen any of the director's previous work. But he had no misgivings about taking a supporting part, despite being one of the biggest stars in films. Nicholson told Ebert,

> My whole career strategy has been to build a base so that I could take the roles I want to play. I'd hate to think that a shorter part might not be available because I was worried about my billing.[5]

Terms of Endearment was a big success at the box office, grossing $3.4 million during its opening weekend, and as late as its eleventh week in release was number one at the box office. It won one Oscar each for Nicholson and MacLaine, and two for Brooks (screenplay and director). Winger was nominated, as was John Lithgow, who played the banker with whom Emma has an affair. Surprisingly, Jeff Daniels's strong portrayal of the difficult Flap character received no nominations.

Most critics praised the film, including Janet Maslin of the *New York Times*, who stated,

> *Terms of Endearment* is a funny, touching, beautifully acted film that covers more territory than it can easily manage. It's the 30-year saga of a mother and daughter; the story of a charmingly eccentric woman who, in her 50s, finally permits herself to fall in love; and the chronicle of a troubled marriage between a young professor and his whimsical bride. It's a comedy, offbeat and lighthearted, then turns painfully and unexpectedly tragic in its final half hour. Garrett Breedlove. This is the character Mr. Brooks has added to the story,

and as played by Jack Nicholson he becomes a masterly comic invention, with a magnificent repulsiveness that Mr. Nicholson turns into pure hilarity. Garrett is capable of making a mere lunch invitation sound amazingly obscene, and when he flirts with Aurora over the hedge that separates their houses, he threatens to ooze over into her yard. Miss MacLaine's deliberate coolness makes her a perfect foil for this sort of thing, and her scenes with Mr. Nicholson are among the film's most delightful.[6]

Despite being known as a tearjerker, *Terms of Endearment* offers a lot of humor as it leads up to its tragic final act. Much of that is due to Nicholson playing his rough but charismatic character. He has real chemistry with MacLaine, who often played similarly fiery characters. About the character she played, MacLaine recalled for the Associated Press upon her eightieth birthday in 2014,

> I adore her. I would like her on my tombstone. My favorite part. It wasn't really acting. I'm kind of like her.[7]

Nicholson continues to amaze with his ability to easily transition from yelling and acting crazy to delivering a more low-key bit of dialogue. The movie is much more than the "chick flick" many people categorize it as being. It effectively explores deeper emotions from characters that are solidly developed throughout the film. As a result, the ending doesn't come off as too sentimental or overly manipulative.

Satisfied with his Oscar-winning performance in a supporting role, it would be almost two more years after the release of *Terms of Endearment* before Jack Nicholson appeared in another movie.

PRIZZI'S HONOR

(1985, 20th Century Fox)

★ ★ ★ ★

Director: John Huston
Screenplay: Janet Roach, Richard Condon, based on the novel by Condon
Producer: John Foreman. *Cinematographer:* Andrzej Bartkowiak. *Editors:* Kaja
  Fehr, Rudi Fehr
Cast: Jack Nicholson (Charley Partanna); Kathleen Turner (Irene Walker);
  Robert Loggia (Eduardo Prizzi); John Randolph (Angelo Partanna);
  William Hickey (Don Corrado Prizzi); Anjelica Huston (Maerose
  Prizzi); Lawrence Tierney (Lt. Hanley); CCH Pounder (Peaches); Ann
  Selepegno (Amalia); Vic Polizos (Phil); Dick O'Neill (Bluestone); Sully
  Boyar (Casco Vascone); Antonia Vasquez (Theresa); Tomasino Baratta
  (Opera Singer); John Calvani (Bodyguard); Murray Staff (Gallagher);
  Joseph Ruskin (Marxie Heller); Ray Serra (Bocca); Seth Allen (Alvin
  Gomsky); Dominic Barto (Presto Ciglione); Teddi Siddall (Beulah); Ray
  Inannicelli, Tom Signorelli (Photographers); Stanley Tucci (Soldier);
  Michael Sabin (Charley at Seventeen); Marlene D. Williams (Mrs.
  Calhane); Vince Cecere (Cheech)
Released: June 14, 1985
Specs: 130 minutes; color
Availability: DVD (MGM)

Prizzi's Honor is another very good film and with a lot of important elements. First, it is one of the last films directed by John Huston, who began
his career with the classic *The Maltese Falcon* (1941). Now suffering from
emphysema, Huston would direct one more film, *The Dead*, in 1987, the
year of his passing. Second, it allows Jack Nicholson to once again reach as
an actor, playing a character that is much different than his usual screen
persona. Finally, it uses the gangster theme, massively popular in the 1930s
and made popular again after the *Godfather* films in the 1970s, and plays
it for dry comedy.

Jack plays Charley Partanna, a hit man who works for a wealthy mob family, the Prizzis. He answers directly to his own father, Angelo, who is Don
Corrado Prizzi's trusted confidante. At a family wedding, Charley meets
and falls for Irene, an attractive woman who turns out to be a fellow assas-
sin, and Charley has a contract to murder her husband. Despite this odd
beginning, Charley and Irene eventually fall in love and later get married
in Mexico. While teaming up for a kidnapping, Charley and Irene successfully carry out their plan for the most part, but Irene ends up having to kill
a woman visitor as she leaves the elevator. She turns out to be an officer's
wife. This hampers the Prizzi family's business relationship with the police.

Nicholson and Kathleen Turner as married assassins in *Prizzi's Honor. 20th Century Fox Film
Corporation / Photofest © 20th Century Fox Film Corporation*

Different factions of the Prizzi family want either Irene or Charley taken out. Unfortunately, Irene is assigned to assassinate Charley, while Charley is separately hired to murder Irene.

When Irene is first assigned to kill Charley, she comes to him. He is more insulted than anything else. It is explained that her assignment was given by someone who did not realize they were acquainted, much less married, and "he wanted the best," as if that made everything okay. Dominic, the man who assigns Irene to do this, is one of the Prizzi sons, but his decision so appalls Charley's father that one of the other brothers arranges a hit on Dominic to be done by Charley.

It is a financial situation that results in Charley being assigned to kill Irene. Irene wants a great sum of money from the Prizzis, believing that they owe it to her. They patiently tell Charley that Irene has to go. Charley initially rebels against the idea, but finally realizes that his work for the family is his world, even more so than his wife. He agrees to the hit. He calls Irene and says the Prizzis have agreed to give her the money. Charley's reassurance that "everything is gonna be okay" arouses her suspicions, and she realizes her situation. She flees to California. Charley follows her. They reconnect happily, but as Charley sleeps, Irene pulls a gun and shoots at him. She just misses him as Charley rises up and throws a knife that goes right into her throat, killing her. Charley returns to his work for the family. He misses Irene, but takes some solace in reconnecting with an old girlfriend, Maerose Prizzi, who had been on the outs with the family but recently returned in good graces after revealing Irene's financial double cross against the organization. When Charley phones and asks Maerose to dinner, she asks, "Me, you, and Irene?" Charley says, "No, Irene had to go away." Maerose smiles big and says, "Charley, just tell me where you want to meet!"

Upon first reading the script, the actors didn't initially realize it was supposed to be a comedy. It has such of a dark, off-kilter approach to its humor, it wasn't until they reached certain points of dialogue in the initial reading that the actors found the script funny. During the kidnapping scene, Irene is holding a doll that is supposed to represent a baby. She throws it at one of the bodyguards during the kidnapping, expecting him to catch it, but he does not. Afterward she says to Charley, "What kind of creep wouldn't catch a baby? If it was real it'd be crippled for life!" Reportedly everyone laughed at that point of the script during the reading and recognized the screenplay's quirky humor. The studio had its own problems with this project. They felt that not even an actor the caliber of Jack Nicholson could make a man who is hired to kill his own wife likable. They also missed the point that this was a dark comedy where such a situation would not be taken seriously. At one point, Charley ponders his assignment by saying aloud to himself, "Do I marry her? Do I ice her? Which one of these?" The absurdity was determined to be a bit too edgy for mass audiences to find amusing.

Critics seemed to be in on the joke without a problem. Pauline Kael stated in the *New Yorker*,

> This John Huston picture has a ripe and daring comic tone. It revels voluptuously in the murderous finagling of the members of a Brooklyn Mafia family, and rejoices in their scams. It's like *The Godfather* acted out by *The Munsters*. Jack Nicholson's average-guyness as Charley, the clan's enforcer, is the film's touchstone: this is a baroque comedy about people who behave in ordinary ways in grotesque circumstances, and it has the juice of everyday family craziness in it.[1]

Sheila Benson in the *Los Angeles Times* stated,

> To say the film is the treasure of the year would be to badmouth it in this disastrous season. *Prizzi's Honor* would be the vastly original centerpiece of a *great* year. . . . At the center of the action is Jack Nicholson as Charley Partanna, the Prizzis' principal hit man. You want someone iced, you call Cholly: very efficient, not a creep—no ice picks, just *va voom* an' the problem is gone.[2]

Jack Nicholson's challenging characterization does not appear to be steeped in any of his other quirky performances. This character is a thick-tongued, ponderous murderer whose skills at hits belie his general stupidity. John Huston directed Nicholson's performance by regularly reminding him that the character he was playing was stupid. Thus, Nicholson carefully kept his natural wit and intelligence from seeping into the role. Charley is as much of an intellectual moron as he is a dangerous, wily hit man. Nicholson's performance is so offbeat that it very effectively embellishes the dark comedy of the screenplay. Even his voice sounds nothing like his usual delivery (actress and playwright Julie Bovasso helped Nicholson master effective Brooklynese).

This performance is interesting in that it is another that is completely different from anything Nicholson had done before. Of course, this is far from the first time he'd done comedy, but his role differs from, for instance, the purely silly *Goin' South* in that his character doesn't have an intellectual sense of humor; he's just kind of dumb, and comes off just as you would imagine a stereotypical gangster hit man might. Perhaps a comic version of

Lenny Montana's characterization of Luca Brasi, whose fumbling manner in *The Godfather* was not unlike Charley Partanna.

While Kathleen Turner is quite effective as the attractive, waspy Irene, it is Anjelica Huston, the director's daughter, in the much smaller role as Maerose, who registers most effectively. She carefully embodies the role of the family rebel, the blackest sheep within an entire brood of black sheep, who continues to harbor a love for Charley. Her pointing out Irene's danger to the organization does result in the competition being killed. She, therefore, might be the most dangerous character in the narrative. *Variety* stated,

> Even more monstrous, in a deceptive way, is the character played by Anjelica Huston, who is the black sheep of the powerful clan, but who maneuvers the plot in insidious ways, all of them tied to the fact that she harbors a lost love for Nicholson.[3]

Other critics also took notice, and despite *Prizzi's Honor* receiving several Oscar nominations, including Best Picture, Ms. Huston was the only one to win. It was the second time John Huston directed a family member to an Oscar-winning performance. The second was his father, Walter Huston, for *The Treasure of the Sierra Madre* (1948). Nicholson told *Film Comment*,

> I have been silently hoping for Anjelica's success as an actress, and I'm very happy that it is beginning in a picture we worked on together. *Prizzi* should be a career-maker for her; she is flawless in it. And in the real world, it was a big deal for her and John to work so successfully together.[4]

John Huston surrounded himself with old friends as he directed this movie. Script supervisor Meta Wilde had been his script girl way back on *The Maltese Falcon*. Editor Rudi Fehr, who'd worked with Huston on *Key Largo* (1948), came out of retirement to work with his daughter Kaja on *Prizzi's Honor*. And, finally, when seventy-nine-year-old John Huston was nominated for an Oscar as Best Director, he was the oldest one to have received that honor, a record that still stands at the time of this writing. Nicholson recalled for *Film Comment*,

> John camera cuts. If you only do one take you don't really know what you did. You don't get to refine it. You come home and think of the 35 things you might've thrown in the stew. When a director shoots several takes, you eventually find his rhythm and try to come up to the boil together. But with John Huston everybody's got to be ready to go right away. But there were never

any problems. Everyone had such respect for him that no one wanted to be the fly-in-the-ointment, so to speak.[5]

Prizzi's Honor was not expected to be a big box office success, so the studio put it out quickly as a summer release. It became quite a big hit via star power and eventual word of mouth, as well as critical acclaim. While its hefty budget was in excess of $16 million, it took in nearly $30 million at the box office.

Terms of Endearment was made after Nicholson had been away from movie screens for nearly two years, and just as much time passed before he made *Prizzi's Honor*. He had been given scripts regularly, but none interested him, and he was now a big enough star that he could work whenever he wanted. The layoff between *The Border* and *Terms of Endearment* had proved that time did not hamper his box office success. Nicholson was offered the role of Ernest Hemingway, which he turned down, and the film then became a forgettable TV movie. He was also offered the Eliot Ness role in Brian De Palma's *The Untouchables* (1987), which he also turned down, that role going to Kevin Costner. He found *Prizzi's Honor* among a pile of scripts that he was going through, and chose it as his next project. Talk of a possible sequel to *Chinatown* interested him. Talk of a possible sequel to *Terms of Endearment* did not.

After completing *Prizzi's Honor*, Nicholson returned to movie screens a year later in Nora Ephron's comedy *Heartburn*. The chance to once again work with director Mike Nichols and play opposite an actress like Meryl Streep both interested Nicholson, while Paramount Pictures felt that a writer, director, and two stars of their caliber would ensure tremendous box office success. The box office was not bad. The film came out in July 1986 and earned $5,783,079 during its opening weekend, ranking number two at the box office behind *Aliens*. *Heartburn* eventually grossed a total of $25,314,189 in the United States. However, this seriocomic semi-biographical film, based on Nora Ephron's book chronicling her marriage to reporter Carl Bernstein, did nothing to advance Jack Nicholson's career.

Nicholson's next big hit had him once again in a supporting role, only this time in a pivotal role as the devil himself.

THE WITCHES OF EASTWICK

(1987, Warner Bros.)

★ ★ ★ ½

Director: George Miller
Screenplay: Michael Cristofer, based on the novel by John Updike
Producers: Neil Canton, Peter Guber, Jon Peters. *Cinematographer:* Vilmost
    Zsigmond. *Editors:* Hubert C. de la Bouillerie, Richard Francis-Bruce
Cast: Jack Nicholson (Daryl Van Horne), Cher (Alexandra), Susan Sarandon
    (Jane), Michelle Pfeiffer (Sukie), Veronica Cartwright (Felicia), Richard
    Jenkins (Clyde), Keith Jochim (Walter), Carel Struycken (Fidel), Helen
    Lloyd Breed (Mrs. Biddle), Carol Struzik (Carol Melford), Becca Lish
    (Mrs. Neff)
Released: June 12, 1987
Specs: 118 minutes; Technicolor
Availability: DVD (Warner)

In *The Witches of Eastwick*, Jack Nicholson's character of Daryl Van Horne
is supposed to be the devil himself. And the way Nicholson plays him is yet
another culmination of elements from past characters. In each of his movies, Nicholson defines his screen role by drawing from appropriate traits
from past characters. This is again evident in *The Witches of Eastwick*, and
he appears to be having an especially good time doing so.

Daryl Van Horne descends upon the picturesque town of Eastwick,
Rhode Island, where three female friends—Alex, Jane, and Sukie, all

abandoned by their men by divorce, death, or desertion—are living without the knowledge that they are, in fact, witches. Van Horne is a wealthy sculptor who disrupts the town by purchasing landmarks and attracting the people with his wily personality. The only one who exhibits suspicion is the devoutly religious Felicia and her newspaper editor husband, Clyde.

Daryl seduces each of the three witches, bringing out their witching abilities, and they agree to share in his affections. The time they spend at his mansion results in negative gossip from Felicia and Clyde, causing them to become outcasts to the town. Daryl puts a spell on Felicia where cherries appear in her mouth whenever one of the witches has one at his mansion. She begins choking and vomiting, her erratic, overbearing behavior becoming so violent that her husband kills her. This shocks the witches, so they back off from Daryl. He responds by casting spells on each woman related to her greatest fear (Alex wakes up in a bed full of snakes, Jane starts to suddenly age rapidly, Suki is wrought with terrible pain). The witches then respond by creating a voodoo doll of Daryl and forcing him to suffer. Eventually they throw the doll into a fire and he vanishes. The film ends with the women now living in Daryl's mansion. When Daryl's image appears on the television, they switch the TV off.

Because Jack Nicholson's films had set such a high bar, a wicked comedy like *The Witches of Eastwick* seems a bit less impressive in the wake of something like *The Shining*. However, the cast is strong and the performances are effectively over the top as well as sufficiently subtle when necessary. Cher, Susan Sarandon, and Michelle Pfeiffer play characters that are very different from each other but hold the common bond of witchcraft and their connection to Daryl. When he seduces each, he does so with careful pragmatism, appealing to the base nature of each individual, including her specific interests and personality. His manipulative style is based on the stories of Satan, who is biblically described as a master manipulator. He is effective. In order to release Suki from her pain, Alex goes to see Daryl, and he once again uses his power of manipulation, pleading with her to return with the other girls into the situation they'd had prior to Felicia's death. The women outsmart him, though, and manage to retain enough elements (hair follicles, etc.) to create the voodoo doll.

While there are elements of horror, there are some very funny scenes in *The Witches of Eastwick*. Daryl has a dry wit about him that is consistently amusing. In an early scene when a dull headmaster is giving an outdoor speech, all three girls exhibit boredom at the same time, and a rainstorm breaks up the assembly. As the audience runs inside for cover, the headmaster continues to yell his speech in the rain, undaunted by the elements.

The highlight of the film's comic element is when the witches perform their voodoo magic on Daryl. During a pleasant visit to an ice cream parlor, he screams in pain from the voodoo curse, punching through the glass enclosure and putting his fist into a bucket of ice cream. The confused vendor calmly asks, "Is everything okay?" The witches eat cherries, and the cherries choke Daryl in the same manner as they had affected Felicia.

Nicholson's physical performance is extraordinary throughout. It begins as he sprawls on a bed in satin pajamas, looking both evil and seductive at the same time. It concludes with a ravaged devil, after having endured the voodoo spells, running through town hunched over and battered, and then driving rapidly until he reaches the mansion where the women are. His eyeballs are raised toward his forehead, his mouth is open to a snarl, his hair is sticking out from all sides, and his limbs are transforming into beastly paws. Nicholson is at one with the visual effects, and it is his performance that makes these scenes exciting, the effects only enhancing the imagery.

Director George Miller had helmed the *Mad Max* films (and would later direct the twenty-first-century versions when the franchise was revived, earning an Oscar nomination). So he was adept at maintaining a literate narrative while utilizing visual effects. However, his choice for Veronica Cartwright to play so far over the top as Felicia sometimes disrupts the power of the character. She responds to most situations with screaming, screeching, and sputtering to the point where her impact is lessened in the narrative, and she never appears to be a threat worth acknowledging. It never completely registers why she is such a significant opposition that Daryl deems her death necessary. Felicia's eccentricity might have been more effective if the director allowed her to become gradually crazier throughout the film, but her initial eccentricities give way to full-blown wildness rather quickly. Cartwright, an excellent actress playing against type, does her best under the circumstances.

The best thing about *The Witches of Eastwick* is Jack Nicholson's bravura performance. Its aforementioned culmination stems from the actor's use of traits that he'd refined over what was now a long, successful screen career. The mental patient in *One Flew over the Cuckoo's Nest*; the madman in *The Shining*; the manipulative, charismatic loner in *Terms of Endearment* are all represented in Daryl Van Horne. And since nearly every Nicholson role had an edge, it is natural for him to be cast as the edgiest character of all (Bill Murray was briefly considered for the role, which would have offered a completely different perspective). Nicholson takes a character who should be unlikable and makes him charming. Even by the end of the film, it is difficult to dislike him entirely.

Before agreeing to do *The Witches of Eastwick*, Nicholson was offered the role opposite Bette Midler in Paul Mazursky's *Down and Out in Beverly Hills* (1986), but he turned it down (it went to Nick Nolte). He was also offered the leading role opposite Dustin Hoffman in Barry Levinson's *Rain Man* (1988), but he realized the role Hoffman had was really the standout part and turned that down as well (when the film was eventually made, Tom Cruise was cast). Director Miller wanted Robert De Niro, but he was busy with another project. Once Nicholson signed on (for a reported $6 million and a percentage of the film's gross), Anjelica Huston wanted to play one of the witches. Nicholson's influence was not enough to make that happen, and this hampered their already shaky relationship.

Apparently the egos of the three leading actresses did not allow the same camaraderie on the set as their characters had in the film. Director George Miller, who was from Australia, did not quite know how to handle egocentric American actresses, and his special effects ideas were causing budgetary problems. Producer Peter Gruber considered removing Miller from the project, but Nicholson threatened to leave as well if that happened. Gruber then entrusted Nicholson to assist the director in not going over budget while acting as peacemaker among the three actresses. Cher recalled for the *Philadelphia Daily News*,

> Jack has a fondness for women as a species. He would make us our lunch every day. "OK, witches! Come on. Where are my witches?" And he would put it down in front of us and dish it out and serve us. We felt so protected by Jack that we really wanted to be around him almost at all times.[1]

The Witches of Eastwick opened in the summer of 1987 and eventually made $64 million at the box office after a budget of $22 million. It was the tenth-highest-grossing film of the year. While audiences and most critics liked it, some reviewers were underwhelmed. Janet Maslin in the *New York Times* stated,

> Beneath the surface charm there is too much confusion, and the charm itself is gone long before the film is over. Though the performers are eminently watchable, the sight of all three women flouncing naughtily in their lingerie, or marching about in unison, effectively renders the whole thing rather silly. In any case, none of them seem a match for Mr. Nicholson's self-proclaimed "horny little devil." As battles of the sexes go, this is barely a scrimmage.[2]

Despite the fact that her review did not appear to fully appreciate the film's humor or effectiveness, Maslin did point out that Jack Nicholson was its strongest factor. And, as time has gone by, *The Witches of Eastwick* has maintained a solid base of appreciation from film buffs and Jack Nicholson's fans.

Shortly after the release of *The Witches of Eastwick*, John Huston took ill while working as an actor on what would be his last film, the TV movie *Mister Corbett's Ghost*, which was being directed by his son Danny. Huston had recently completed directing *The Dead*, which was to be his final theatrical film. Jack Nicholson flew to the location where Huston was hospitalized and remained with him until he died on August 28, 1987, at the age of eighty-one. A saddened Jack Nicholson later told Peter Bogdanovich in an interview for the German *Suddeutsche Zeitung Magazin*, "For a certain period of my life I knew the greatest guy alive."[3]

IRONWEED

(1987, TriStar)

★ ★ ★ ★

Director: Hector Babenco
Screenplay: William Kennedy, based on his novel
Producers: Keith Barish, Marcia Nasatir. *Cinematographer:* Lauro Escorel.
   Editor: Anne Goursaud
Cast: Jack Nicholson (Francis Phelan), Meryl Streep (Helen Archer), Carroll
   Baker (Annie Phelan), Michael O'Keefe (Billy Phelan), Diane Venora
   (Peg), Fred Gwynne (Oscar), Margaret Whitton (Katrina), Tom
   Waits (Rudy), Jake Denel (Pee Wee), Nathan Lane (Harold), James
   Gammon (Reverend Chester), Will Zahrn (Rowdy Dick), Laura
   Esterman (Nora), Joe Grifasi (Jack), Hy Anzell (Rosskam), Bethel Leslie
   (Librarian), Richard Hamilton (Donovan), Black Eyed Susan (Clara),
   Priscilla Smith (Sandra), James Dukas (Phinny), Ted Levine (Pocono
   Pete), Martin Patterson (Foxy Phil Tooker)
Released: December 18, 1987
Specs: 143 minutes; color
Availability: DVD (Lions Gate)

After the completion of *The Witches of Eastwick* and prior to starting *Ironweed*, Jack Nicholson did an unbilled cameo as a newscaster in James L. Brooks's *Broadcast News*, which starred William Hurt, Holly Hunter, and Albert Brooks. Thus, *Ironweed* was one of three films in which Jack Nicholson appeared that were released during 1987.

Despite the fact that their last pairing, *Heartburn*, had been a disappointment at the box office the year before, Jack Nicholson was reteamed with Meryl Streep for *Ironweed*. They play Francis and Helen, a couple of alcoholic drifters who meet up in 1938 Albany, New York, which had been Francis's home town. A former major league baseball player, Francis ran away from his wife and son after dropping his other son and killing him. While in Albany, Francis reconnects with Helen and also tries to reconnect with his wife and child, whom he has not seen in twenty years.

With this premise, *Ironweed* explores guilt and anguish as well as loyalty and fairness within characters who have chosen to check out of life and wallow in alcoholic despair. Streep's character of Helen is a former singer who is inspired, by Fran's return home, to attempt a return to singing. Fran is surrounded by death, in images and the tasks he performs. The job he secures to pay for his drinking is grave digging. He visits the grave of the son he dropped. He is haunted by images of two men he's killed. When Fran reconnects with his family and first meets his grandson, he is unable to wrap his mind around the situation. He wants to be with them but remains overwhelmed by guilt from the past. Helen is exploring her own possibilities and limitations.

Meryl Streep and Nicholson in the film adaptation of William Kennedy's Pulitzer Prize–winning novel *Ironweed*. TriStar / Photofest © TriStar

Ironweed is one of the lesser known Jack Nicholson movies, but it is essential to his film career due to both him and Streep being nominated for Oscars (neither won). William Kennedy's Pulitzer Prize–winning novel was a good source for this Depression-era drama, but some believed the movie did not, according to Michael Ryan in *People* magazine, "achieve the metaphysical transcendence of the book."[1] In that same article, writer Kennedy explains that Gene Hackman, Jason Robards, and Sam Shepard were all interested in playing Francis, but Kennedy wanted Nicholson. However, he wasn't completed prepared for Nicholson's input beyond acting. According to *People*,

> Kennedy doesn't try to hide the fact that his *Ironweed* screenplay had liberal input from its stars. Nicholson himself is a former screenwriter. He has vigorous opinions on the subject and no temerity about expressing them. "Sometimes I made the changes he asked, sometimes I didn't," says Kennedy. They disagreed over a scene in which Francis has a fight with Helen on the street. "They clinch, and she says, 'You gonna hit me?' and he says, 'Nah, I love you some.' Jack didn't want to say 'I love you.' He didn't think you could say 'I love you' in the movies anymore." In the end, "Jack did it the way it was written." Kennedy says that Nicholson was concerned about playing what he considered his "most complex role" to date. "Jack has never gone as far out, he's never had to be this destitute a character."

Nicholson met the challenge effectively, and by the way Kennedy describes the actor's input, it appears he delineated the written character along the lines of his own established approach. When comparing Fran in *Ironweed* to Daryl in *The Witches of Eastwick*, the difference in Nicholson's approach is palpable. Fran is much more subdued, much more haunted, far less in control. Director George Miller had wanted over-the-top performances in *The Witches of Eastwick*. Director Hector Babenco, who'd also helmed the acclaimed *Kiss of the Spider Woman* (1986), preferred a subtler approach. So did Kennedy's written work. Nicholson responded appropriately while also enjoying the level of creative input his star status allowed him.

One of the rumors regarding the production of *Ironweed* dealt with an alleged fling between Nicholson and Streep. They did develop a closeness on the set, perhaps as a response to their having some alleged difficulty getting along while filming *Heartburn*. But the rumors about their connection while shooting *Ironweed* have persisted, although both actors have denied it. In any case, their on-screen chemistry is far more effective in this film than it had been in *Heartburn*, where a lackluster script gave them less opportunity than William Kennedy's more insightful screenplay.

Critics were impressed with both actors and noted that *Ironweed* was a departure for each of them. Roger Ebert wrote,

> Nicholson and Streep play drunks in *Ironweed*, and actors are said to like to play drunks, because it gives them an excuse for overacting. But there is not much visible "acting" in this movie; the actors are too good for that.[2]

Janet Maslin of the *New York Times* wrote,

> Meryl Streep, as ever, is uncanny. Miss Streep uses the role of Helen as an opportunity to deliver a stunning impersonation of a darty-eyed, fast-talking woman of the streets, an angry, obdurate woman with great memories and no future. There isn't much more to the film's Helen than this, and indeed the character may go no deeper, but she's a marvel all the same. Behind the runny, red-rimmed eyes, the nervous chatter and the haunted expression, Miss Streep is even more utterly changed than her costar, and she even sings well. The sequence in which Helen entertains the real and imagined patrons of a bar room with a rendition of "He's Me Pal" is a standout.[3]

Sheila Benson of the *Los Angeles Times* stated,

> Nicholson's performance doesn't whimper for our approval, and it carries some of the intensely ironic Irish humor that runs in a vein through the book. The back-and-forth between Phelan and Tom Waits' Rudy provides some the film's greatest joys. And there are fine moments, too, in Phelan's scene with the old, randy rag and bone man (Hy Anzell) whose route takes Phelan dangerously close to home turf.
>
> And the gentleness, the raffish gallantry that he shows for Helen is all the more touching when we realize that she is literally dying because he is running away from her too. He will find a car for her to sleep in, but ignore the dear price she'll have to pay to a grizzled alcoholic for the shelter.[4]

This movie was a great opportunity for Nicholson to show another layer to his acting abilities, that while he could play a very manic, over-the-top character, he was just as adept at going in the opposite direction. Streep's character is much more over the top here, but effectively. It's wonderful to see one of the era's best actors play against one of its best actresses.

Nicholson had, by now, decided that he wanted to play a character with different qualities in each subsequent movie. *The Witches of Eastwick* had been over the top. *Ironweed* had been more concentrated and subdued. So,

Nicholson's next choice was to play the flamboyant Joker in Tim Burton's cinematic take on *Batman*. Nicholson accepted yet another supporting role, realizing that there was a great deal he could do with the character, inspired by the delightfully campy portrayal by Cesar Romero on the 1960s *Batman* television series. When the casting of Jack Nicholson was announced for the role, prerelease publicity generated a great deal of interest in how Nicholson would approach the part, especially since director Burton was telling the press that he intended to be closer to the darkness of the original comic book character and not produce something campy like the TV series. The Joker, however, is still a flamboyant character. And it was just the role for Jack Nicholson at this point in his career.

21

BATMAN

(1989, Warner Bros.)

★ ★ ★ ★

Director: Tim Burton
Screenplay: Sam Hamm, Warren Skaaren. *Characters:* Bob Kane, Bill Finger
Producers: Peter Guber, Jon Peters. *Cinematographer:* Roger Pratt. *Editor:* Ray
    Lovejoy. *Music:* Danny Elfman
Cast: Michael Keaton (Batman/Bruce Wayne), Jack Nicholson (Joker/Jack
    Napier), Kim Basinger (Vicki Vale), Robert Wuhl (Alexander Knox),
    Pat Hingle (Commissioner Gordon), Billy Dee Williams (Harvey Dent),
    Michael Gough (Alfred), Jack Palance (Grissom), Jerry Hall (Alicia
    Hunt), Tracey Walter (Bob), Lee Wallace (Mayor), William Hootkins
    (Lt. Eckhardt), Christopher Fairbank (Nic), Kit Hollerbach (Becky),
    Hugo Blick (Young Jack), Charles Roskilly (Young Bruce), David Baxt
    (Dr. Wayne), Sharon Holm (Mrs. Wayne), Lee Wallace (Mayor)
Released: June 23, 1989
Specs: 126 minutes; Technicolor
Availability: DVD (Warner)

In the wake of the popular 1960s television series on which actor Adam
West played a campy, tongue-in-cheek version of the caped crusader from
DC comics, filmmaker Tim Burton chose to instead make a film based on
the original dark comic book character. However, Burton's choice to film
Batman as more serious than camp does not mean the comic's inherent

campy elements were completely eschewed. Nicholson provides a delight-fully over-the-top portrayal of the Joker, which nicely counterpoints Mi-chael Keaton's deadly serious turn as the caped crusader. It is a dynamic that works perfectly. Burton then surrounds the central characters with a growling William Hootkins as Lieutenant Eckhardt; a wisecracking Robert Wuhl as reporter Alexander Knox; a hard-edged Pat Hingle as Commis-sioner Gordon; a gruff, commanding Jack Palance as Carl Grissom; a flashy Billy Dee Williams as Harvey Dent; and an enthusiastic Kim Basinger as Vicki Vale. These capable actors are effective in bringing comic book char-acters to life because each is committed to his or her role and responds well to Burton's direction. Burton's vision as a filmmaker is dark, atmospheric, and dramatic, but he still realizes there are established traits within each character from the comics that he must address with some enhancement. And it is Jack Nicholson who once again steals the film in another support-ing role.

Jack Napier is a criminal who has connected with mob boss Grissom's girl. This is just as an increased police presence has targeted Grissom and his mob. Grissom sends Napier on a robbery mission at a chemical plant and sets him up to be killed, with crooked Lieutenant Eckhardt as an ac-complice. Batman shows up to foil the robbery; Napier realizes the setup and shoots Eckhardt. He attempts to shoot Batman, but ends up plum-meting into a vat of chemicals. They destroy the nerves in his body and face, which is frozen into an evil grin. Napier snaps upon seeing himself in a mirror and becomes a crazed, giggling "Joker" who seeks both revenge and control. He kills Grissom and takes over the mob. Meanwhile, Knox and Vale are investigating Batman, and Joker wants to use them to obtain information, realizing Batman is his true nemesis.

Burton quickly establishes that this isn't an origin story. We get an idea through flashbacks of how Bruce Wayne became Batman, but the whole point of the movie doesn't revolve around him actually becoming Batman. It is, however, the only movie to tell of the Joker's origin. Normally, the Joker is such an enigma that explaining so much of his past would dimin-ish his character, but it works here because it effectively sets up the rivalry between Joker and Batman. They play off each other perfectly: they're both freaks living on the outside of society, and in a way, one can't exist without the other.

Burton's establishing scenes introduce not only the characters but also the setting of a crime-ridden city where the police, even with greater pres-ence, are ineffective. Keaton's seriousness in the title role extends to the Bruce Wayne character. When Vicki and Knox visit his palatial mansion,

Michael Keaton as the caped crusader and Nicholson as the crown prince of crime in Tim Burton's *Batman*. *Warner Bros.* / *Photofest © Warner Bros.*

Knox quips, "Can I have a grand?" Once their business has concluded, Wayne matter-of-factly gives closing orders to his butler, Alfred, including "and give Knox a grand." The dynamic between Keaton and Knox is further extended in the Batman-Joker relationship. Nicholson presented Napier as low key and subdued, but the Joker is the polar opposite. As over the top as his devil character in *The Witches of Eastwick*, the Joker, like Satan, is a role tailor-made for Nicholson's edgy, off-kilter approach.

The Joker's feelings toward Batman are a combination of contempt and admiration. He sits in his home and laments to his underlings, "How can a man dressed as a bat get all of my press?" He creates a deadly chemical called Smilex and places it in several hygiene products so that women die, sometimes laughing themselves to death. They are found with frozen smiles not unlike the Joker's face. It is an attempt to draw Batman out of hiding so he can be confronted. Bruce Wayne watches, with intent, the weird commercials in which the Joker advertises the products he has contaminated with Smilex.

Burton likes to dwell on the Joker's playful nature, especially in a scene where he destroys priceless paintings in a museum with his flunkies. They dance about with a Prince song on the soundtrack, soon confronting a captured Vicki where the Joker introduces himself as "the first fully functioning homicidal artist" who wants "[his] face on the one dollar bill." When Batman comes in and rescues her, the Joker is more impressed with the gadgetry he uses, exclaiming, "Where does he get those wonderful toys?"

The film alternates effectively from Bruce Wayne's low-key seriousness, to Batman's heroics, to the Joker's histrionics. The narrative remains basic to the characters, and it is they who allow the story to progress. In a book about Nicholson, it is his work on which we focus.

By this point in his career, Nicholson was fully established as a screen actor with recognizable traits. He explores the Joker character by not only offering the wackiness of the character's obsessions, but also reaching into the underlying psychology of a criminal who was betrayed and disfigured, and continues to be merely a distraction compared to the massive interest in a dazzling crime fighter. Nicholson recalled in an interview with *MTV News*,

> Well, the Joker comes from my childhood. That's how I got involved with it in the first place. It's a part I always thought I should play. Tim Burton's a genius. He had the right take on it. That's why I did the movie. I did the movie based on a single conversation with him. We both come from the cartoon world originally. We had similar ideas. Tim said [the Joker] should have a humorous dark side to him. Burton is one of the great moviemakers. I think the world of him. He's the most unassuming man. And he doesn't feel pressure. That's what I love about him. Once he's in there, he's smiling making the movie. That's it![1]

Nicholson was paid $6 million and a percentage of the profits, which came to around $75 million. His contract carefully specified the number of hours he was entitled to have off each day, from the time he left the set to the time he reported back for filming. He was also allowed off for Los Angeles Lakers home games. When promoting his later super hero movie *Birdman*, Michael Keaton recalled for Jimmy Kimmel the sight of a fully costumed Joker hunched over a television watching Laker games.

The fact that Keaton remains carefully low key throughout the movie allows Nicholson's more elaborate portrayal to stand out. In fact, Michael Keaton being cast in the role offered no little controversy at the time. Keaton had established himself most in comedies by this time, his most recent being Tim Burton's outrageously funny *Beetlejuice* (1988). Over fifty thousand protest letters were sent to Warner Bros. regarding the casting of Keaton, while both screenwriter Sam Hamm and Batman creator Bob Kane also questioned the decision. Keaton recalled in a 2011 interview that he had his own misgivings, even while playing the role:

It was an extremely difficult undertaking and Tim is a shy guy, especially back then, and there was so much pressure. We were in England for a long time shooting at Pinewood and it was long, difficult nights in that dank, dark, cold place, and we never knew if it was really working. There was no guarantee that any of this was going to play correctly when it was all said and done. There had never been a movie like it before. There was a lot of risk, too, with Jack looking the way he did and me stepping out in this new way. The pressure was on everybody. You could feel it.[2]

In the twenty-first century, filmmaker Christopher Nolan's approach to the same material, and the late Heath Ledger's interpretation of the Joker, reached a loftier level, both critically and aesthetically, unfortunately overshadowing Burton's film and Nicholson's portrayal. There are so many ways to portray the Joker, from the campiness that Cesar Romero exhibited to the darkness of Heath Ledger. Nicholson strikes the perfect balance between those two extremes. His Joker is flamboyant, but just threatening enough that you can take him seriously as a villain. This role was suited for him perfectly. The costumes and makeup are also very well done and nicely suit the manner in which he portrayed the character.

In fact, it was this Burton film and its massive box office success that were the catalyst for any subsequent superhero films that worked from the DC or Marvel comics franchises. It grossed over a quarter million dollars in its domestic box office and over $400 million worldwide. It also won an Oscar for its art direction. Visually, this is probably the most exciting superhero movie of them all. The design of Gotham City is so intimidating that it feels like another character in the movie. No other movies from this genre feature an environment that makes such an aesthetic impact. The inspiration of Fritz Lang's *Metropolis* is evident. This movie also led into *Batman: The Animated Series*, which launched the line of DC animated movies and TV shows that continued into the twenty-first century.

Despite its box office success, not all of the critics were pleased with the film. For the most part, critics seemed to find that *Batman* was an example of form over substance—the careful art direction and use of special effects were the chief interest, and no strong narrative was there to sustain the filmmaker's visual style. Vincent Canby stated in the *New York Times*,

Not since Lang's *Dr. Mabuse: The Gambler* (1922), *Metropolis* (1926) and *The Last Will of Dr. Mabuse* (1933) have so much talent and money gone into the creation of an expressionistic world so determinedly corrupt. Yet nothing in the movie sustains this vision. The wit is all pictoral. The film meanders mindlessly from one image to the next, as does a comic book.[3]

After completing *Batman*, Jack Nicholson embarked on a pet project. The idea of making *Chinatown* as part of a trilogy finally materialized with a second installment, *The Two Jakes* (1990). And in every area that *Chinatown* succeeded, *The Two Jakes* failed. Nicholson directed, for the last time, and Robert Towne wrote the screenplay, but this tardy sequel was not only a critical failure, it lost nearly $10 million at the box office. The *Washington Post* reviewed it and stated, "At best, the movie comes across as a competently assembled job, a wistful tribute to its former self. At worst, it's wordy, confusing and—here's an ugly word—boring."⁴ This was followed by Bob Rafelson's 1992 comedy *Man Trouble*, an enormous box office flop that was made for $30 million and only grossed a little over $4 million.

Jack Nicholson decided to once again take a smaller role, realizing that a well-written supporting part could be strong enough to stand out despite who might be cast in the lead roles. The result was *A Few Good Men*, in which Nicholson would portray one of the most famous scenes of his entire screen career.

A FEW GOOD MEN

(1992, Columbia)

★ ★ ★ ★ ★

Director: Rob Reiner
Screenplay: Aaron Sorkin, from his play
Producers: David Brown, Rob Reiner, Andrew Scheinman. *Cinematographer:*
    Robert Richardson. *Editors:* Robert Leighton, Steven Nevius
Cast: Tom Cruise (Lt. Daniel Kaffee), Jack Nicholson (Col. Nathan R. Jessup),
    Demi Moore (Lt. Cdr. JoAnne Galloway), Kevin Bacon (Capt. Jack
    Ross), Kiefer Sutherland (Lt. Jonathan Kendrick), Kevin Pollak (Lt.
    Sam Weinberg), James Marshall (Pfc. Louden Downey), J. T. Walsh
    (Lt. Col. Andrew Markinson), Christopher Guest (Dr. Stone), J. A.
    Preston (Judge Randolph), Matt Craven (Lt. Dave Spradling), Wolfgang
    Bodison (Capt. Whitaker), John M. Jackson (Capt. West), Noah Wyle
    (Cpl. Jeffrey Barnes), Cuba Gooding Jr. (Cpl. Hammaker), Lawrence
    Lowe (Bailiff), Josh Malina (Tom), Jan Munroe (Jury Foreman), Ron
    Ostrow (MP), Matthew Saks (David), Harry Caesar (Luther), Michael
    DeLorenzo (Pfc. Santiago), Geoffrey Nauffts (Lt. Sherby), Arthur Senzy
    (Robert McGuire), Aaron Sorkin (cameo in bar)
Released: December 11, 1992
Specs: 138 minutes; Technicolor
Availability: DVD (Sony)

Jack Nicholson was turning down more roles than he was accepting, partly because he was very much in demand and partly because he was dealing with the passing of three close friends. We discussed the passing of John Huston in an earlier chapter. Months after Huston died, Jack was saddened by the passing of his friend Andy Warhol. A few months later, another director friend, Hal Ashby, also died. Nicholson had remained friends with Ashby since they worked together on *The Last Detail*.

As a result, Nicholson wasn't in a hurry to go back to work. He turned down the opportunity to reprise his Joker role in a *Batman* sequel, but was pleased that his old friend Danny DeVito was instead hired to play the Penguin. Jonathan Demme wanted him to play Hannibal Lector in *Silence of the Lambs*, opposite his old *Witches of Eastwick* friend Michelle Pfeiffer, but he also said no to that role. Recast with Anthony Hopkins and Jodie Foster, *Silence of the Lambs* would perform as well as *One Flew over the Cuckoo's Nest* at the Oscars, winning Best Picture, Best Actor, Best Actress, Best Director, and Best Screenplay (adapted). Nicholson also passed on roles in *The Hard Way* (it went to James Woods) and *The Last Boy Scout* (going to Bruce Willis). As discussed in the previous chapter, after the failure of *The Two Jakes*, Jack stayed off screen for two years, returning with the resounding flop *Man Trouble*. But he followed that with one of his most truly iconic roles as Colonel Nathan Jessup in *A Few Good Men*.

Aaron Sorkin was inspired to write the play *A Few Good Men*, about a military lawyer who is assigned to defend two marines up for murder, after speaking to his navy judge advocate general sister over the phone. She was assigned to work on a case of hazing and a subsequent code red. When the twenty-eight-year-old Sorkin went to his bartending job that night, he began writing the outline of the play on cocktail napkins. It became his first play, and the movie rights were sold before it was ever produced on stage.

Broadway actor Stephen Lang wanted to play the role he'd originated on stage, but bankable movie names like James Woods, Robert De Niro, and Al Pacino were also expressing interest in the part. However, director Rob Reiner wanted Jack Nicholson, and offered him $5 million for a supporting role that was shot in only ten days. And although he appears in only four scenes, *A Few Good Men* is still thought of as Jack Nicholson's film, even over its bona fide stars Tom Cruise and Demi Moore, not to mention formidable talent among the supporting roles filled by the likes of Kevin Bacon, J. T. Walsh, Kevin Pollak, Kiefer Sutherland, and Christopher Guest.

Tom Cruise plays Lieutenant Daniel Kaffee, the enthusiastic lawyer who is defending a lance corporal and a private who killed a fellow marine named William Santiago. The murder was the result of a "code red" where soldiers take it upon themselves to exact "violent extrajudicial punishment" for insubordinate behavior. Demi Moore plays Lieutenant Galloway, who suspects a code red has been carried out, but the case is given to Kaffee. When a key witness in the case commits suicide, Kaffee chooses to call Colonel Jessup, the cool-but-volatile commanding officer who kept refusing the murdered man's request for a transfer from the unit. On trial, Jessup admits to calling for the code red and is arrested.

Since Jack Nicholson only plays four scenes in this film, our discussion of his contribution would seem to be limited. In fact, he registers so much in that meager amount of footage and manages to deliver one of the more iconic lines of dialogue in modern cinema, there is a fair amount to discuss.

First, as we have pointed out throughout this text, Nicholson's use of different aspects of previous roles defines his current performance. As we have traced Nicholson's screen performances up to this point, we have examined his various uses of the subdued, the manic, the edgy, and the relaxed and accessible traits of the human psyche. Colonel Jessup is another compendium of these elements. And in four scenes, Nicholson manages to exhibit aspects of each.

His first scene shows Jessup being apprised of the impending investigation, in the comfort of his office. Jessup is grounded, relaxed, and confident in his status and his command. He seems strong, yet pleasant. Tough, yet

Nicholson as arrogant Colonel Jessup in *A Few Good Men*. *Columbia Pictures* / *Photofest* © *Columbia Pictures*

understanding. In charge, but cooperative. We don't see the edgier aspects of the character until the investigating members leave the room and he addresses his immediate underling, Lieutenant Colonel Andrew Markinson, after he believes Markinson says a bit too much in the presence of the investigating lieutenants:

> We go back a while. We went to the Academy together, we were commissioned together, we did our tours in Vietnam together. But I've been promoted up through the chain of command with greater speed and success than you have. Now if that's a source of tension or embarrassment for you, well, I don't give a shit. We're in the business of saving lives, Lieutenant Colonel Markinson. Don't ever question my orders in front of another officer.

Nicholson delivers this line with a low-key snarling tension that comes across quite effectively. We now know that we could be dealing with a rather scary individual.

Jessup is once again in comfortable confines the next time he meets the investigators, enjoying an outdoor meal on a sunny day. He graciously tells the servant the meal was delicious, exhibiting a genuine charm. However, this time, his authority and his edginess become more evident. When Kaffee tries to leave, believing they have enough information for now, Galloway continues to ask pointed, intrusive questions. "She outranks you," Jessup matter-of-factly states. He then continues, "There is nothing on this earth sexier than a woman you have to salute in the morning. Promote 'em all, I say, 'cause this is true: if you haven't gotten a blowjob from a superior officer, well, you're just letting the best in life pass you by." This unsettling bit of dialogue can almost be dismissed in regard to Jessup's age and his military standing, realizing some level of basic sexism might be inherent in that context. But as the lieutenants get up to leave and ask permission to investigate further in areas where Jessup has some authority, he oddly insists that they ask nicely, stating,

> You see Danny, I can deal with the bullets, and the bombs, and the blood. I don't want money, and I don't want medals. What I do want is for you to stand there in that faggoty white uniform and with your Harvard mouth extend me some fucking courtesy. You gotta ask me nicely.

Kaffee does, and is given permission. But further investigation does not produce the results that happen by surprise. Markinson hides in Kaffee's car and pops up, startling the lieutenant as he is driving. Markinson reveals there was a code red. Armed with this information, Kaffee decides to put

Markinson on the stand, promising him immunity. But Markinson commits suicide before that can happen. It is Jessup himself who takes the stand, in one of the most stirring scenes that Jack Nicholson has ever performed.

Nicholson's acting in this scene runs the gamut of his various tools as a seasoned performer. His steely-eyed sense of authority, his complete belief in his military level as to make him untouchable, and his gradual rising anger at the confrontation by this lesser officer culminate at the point where he grandstands and shouts the iconic line "You can't handle the truth" prior to admitting he did order the code red:

> Son, we live in a world that has walls, and those walls have to be guarded by men with guns. Who's gonna do it? You? I have a greater responsibility than you could possibly fathom. You weep for Santiago, and you curse the Marines. You have that luxury. You have the luxury of not knowing what I know. That Santiago's death, while tragic, probably saved lives. And my existence, while grotesque and incomprehensible to you, saves lives. You don't want the truth because deep down in places you don't talk about at parties, you want me on that wall, you need me on that wall. We use words like honor, code, loyalty. We use these words as the backbone of a life spent defending something. You use them as a punchline. I have neither the time nor the inclination to explain myself to a man who rises and sleeps under the blanket of the very freedom that I provide, and then questions the manner in which I provide it. I would rather you just said thank you, and went on your way, Otherwise, I suggest you pick up a weapon, and stand a post. Either way, I don't give a damn what you think you are entitled to.

It is at this point that Kaffee shouts that he wants the truth, Jessup shouts back that he can't handle the truth, but, when asked if he ordered the code red, reveals, "You're goddamn right I did!" Still when Jessup tries to get up and leave the courtroom, regarding it as having been a waste of his time, he is stopped by the judge, surrounded by MPs, and read his rights. Even though he broke military law by issuing the code red, he is unable to comprehend why he is under arrest. He lashes out at Kaffee initially, but calms down, takes his hat, and is escorted away by the MPs.

Tom Cruise recalled in an interview with David Bailey in *GQ* that Nicholson exhibited the character's necessary tension with an economy of movement:

> Playing the scene out, Colonel Jessup as a written character is overpowering, so Jack needed to give him that power. But he understands the camera in such a manner that the power had to come from stillness. So he made his movements so minimal. I could see the motions becoming less and less. So it

becomes like this focus. When it comes to the key point, Jessup doesn't even realize my character has beaten him, but you can see the flicker of Jack's eyes; and it's not calculated, he just understands the power of the frame. That's what makes him a craftsman.[1]

A *Few Good Men* was an enormous success at the box office, grossing over $100 million more than its productions costs. And for his four scenes, Jack Nicholson was nominated for a Best Supporting Actor Oscar and continues to be the actor most associated with the movie despite his small role.

Critical opinion was mostly supportive, and most cited Nicholson's performance as the key to the movie's success. Vincent Canby in the *New York Times* stated,

> The role doesn't have to be big, but if it's good, and if the actor playing it is great, the results can be magically transforming. Witness Jack Nicholson's vicious, funny, superbly reptilian turn in Rob Reiner's entertaining *A Few Good Men*, adapted by Aaron Sorkin from his hit Broadway courtroom drama. Mr. Nicholson . . . in the course of only a handful of scenes, he seems to suffuse the entire production, giving it a weight, density and point that might not otherwise be apparent.[2]

However, Roger Ebert, in the *Chicago Sun-Times*, was underwhelmed:

> Rob Reiner's *A Few Good Men* is one of those movies that tells you what it's going to do, does it, and then tells you what it did. In it, a lawyer played by Tom Cruise previews his courtroom strategy to his friends. The strategy then works as planned—which means that an element of surprise is missing from the most important moment in the movie, and the key scene by Jack Nicholson is undermined—robbed of suspense, and made inevitable.[3]

Aaron Sorkin's strong script and sharp dialogue combine well with Rob Reiner's astute choices as a director, spotlighting each of the actors. But despite the strong cast, where even the smallest roles are filled by familiar faces like Noah Wylie and Cuba Gooding Jr., *A Few Good Men* remains Nicholson's film. He did not win the Oscar, though. This was the year of Clint Eastwood's *Unforgiven*, and Gene Hackman won the Best Supporting Actor award for that film.

For his next film, Nicholson wanted to once again escape into a character who was a series of conflicting complexities. He liked David Mamet's script about union leader Jimmy Hoffa, and he heard his friend Danny DeVito was set to direct but was having trouble casting the lead. Nicholson offered himself for the role. David Mamet had written the screenplay for one of Jack's least interesting flops, the remake of *The Postman Always Rings Twice*, based on James Cain's novel and the 1947 film starring John Garfield. However, Nicholson believed this project would be a much greater success.

23

HOFFA

(1992, 20th Century Fox)

★ ★ ½

Director: Danny DeVito
Screenplay: David Mamet
Producers: Danny DeVito, Caldecot Chubb, Edward R. Pressman.
   Cinematographer: Stephen H. Burum. *Editors:* Lynzee Klingman, Ronald
   Roose
Cast: Jack Nicholson (Jimmy Hoffa), Danny DeVito (Bobby Ciaro), Armand
   Assante (Carol D'Allesandro), J. T. Walsh (Frank Fitzsimmons), John
   C. Reilly (Pete), Kevin Anderson (Bobby Kennedy), John P. Ryan
   (Red Bennett), Robert Prosky (Flynn), Natalija Nogulich (Jo Hoffa),
   Nicholas Pryor (Attorney), Frank Whaley (Kid), Paul Builfoyle (Ted
   Harmon), Karen Young (Young Woman at RTA), Cliff Gorman (Solly
   Stein), Joe Gerco (Foreman), Jim Oschs (Worker), Joe Quasarano
   (Worker), Don Brockett (Police Captain), Dale Young (Father Doyle),
   Tom Finnegan (Teamster President), Richard Schiff (Attorney), Steve
   Witting (Eliot Cookson), Tim Burton (Corpse), Jon Favreau (Extra),
   Bruno Kirby (Nightclub Comic)
Released: December 25, 1992
Specs: 140 minutes; color
Availability: DVD (Fox)

Jack Nicholson had two movies come out in December 1992, *A Few Good Men* and *Hoffa*. *A Few Good Men* featured him in only four scenes, amounting to only ten days' work. The movie had a $40 million budget and grossed nearly $200 million, along with garnering Nicholson an Oscar nomination and an iconic scene ("You can't handle the truth!") despite how little he was in the movie. *Hoffa*, about the Teamsters leader, was a solid starring role about a real-life figure. For that movie, Nicholson received a *Harvard Lampoon* Razzie award nomination for worst performance of the year. *Hoffa* lost nearly $15 million at the box office.

It isn't for lack of effort. Danny DeVito, more noted as a bombastic TV sitcom actor who exceled in fun, raucous comedy, had directed two feature films and several television projects before embarking on this movie, so he was an experienced director. And his direction is quite good. DeVito frames his scenes effectively, his shot composition responds well to the narrative, and his sequences dissolve creatively from one to the next.

Along with the competent direction, David Mamet's script tries to maintain some basis in reality, working from transcripts of actual Senate committee meetings for some scenes. The dialogue is often sharp and witty, defining each character effectively.

Danny DeVito and Nicholson in DeVito's third feature film as a director, *Hoffa*. *20th Century Fox Film Corporation / Photofest © 20th Century Fox Film Corporation*

Finally, Jack Nicholson's performance in the title role gives great attention to detail. He envelops himself in the part so completely, his usual Nicholson screen persona is practically buried by the makeup, the voice, and the mannerisms he uses to be authentic to Hoffa.

The film's first problem is DeVito's feelings about Hoffa and his accomplishments. DeVito presents Hoffa as a towering figure of importance, but avoids any exploration into the man's character. Nicholson's careful detail as an actor is therefore never given enough to investigate more than a superficial look at a man who was a much more complex individual. The budget for this movie reportedly exceeded its limitations during production, causing some corner cutting and a revamping of the schedule, which eventually resulted in a lack of enthusiasm all around. The ingredients from each of the main participants somehow lack the necessary cohesion to make *Hoffa* as strong as its potential.

The film shows James R. Hoffa's rise to the presidency of the Teamsters Union, after being a tireless fighter for worker's rights. He is consistently supported by Bobby Ciaro, his right-hand man and confidante, who loyally supports and assists his ideas and activities. DeVito casts himself as Bobby Ciaro, a fictional character who is supposed to represent several actual Hoffa accomplices. The character is created as a compendium, but it reinvents Hoffa's actual history, as one assumes he had an individual lackey who remained an important part of his life for most of his career. The role is poorly developed and distracts from the central character.

Finally, the ending shows both Hoffa and Ciaro being gunned down in a restaurant parking lot where there were few diners. In fact, Hoffa went missing in 1975 and was eventually declared dead. His remains were never found. Since the restaurant he was actually at on the night he went missing was thriving with activity, it is very unlikely he was killed there. It is far more likely he was taken elsewhere. But nobody knows what actually happened, and the film's speculative revelation rings false.

James R. Hoffa was a champion of the working class who supported unionization for better wages, better hours, insurance benefits, and vacation time. However, he was also involved with underworld activity while being a solid, doting family man. The complexities of such a character should be explored to the point where he does not remain an enigma by the end of the movie.

The Senate committee hearing between Hoffa and Robert Kennedy is taken verbatim from the original court transcripts, and both actors (Kennedy is played by Kevin Anderson) make the actual dialogue come to life. A scene where Ciaro is rebuffed by a club manager and then forces the manager at gunpoint to bring him to the owner's office, only for the manager to stammer apologies once he realizes Ciaro's importance, is less effective because Ciaro is a fictional character. That same problem occurs in another scene where an attempt is made to goad Ciaro into turning on Hoffa and testifying against Hoffa; its effectiveness is thwarted by Ciaro being fictional.

Some attempt is made to show other sides of James Hoffa, including some scenes with his wife and child. But for the most part it is a semi-factual account of his union activities, dotted with fictional characters and supported by accurate renditions of actual events. Its importance to Nicholson's career is due to his escaping so completely into the character, losing his noted screen persona within the charismatic figure of another individual. The makeup work in *Hoffa* was nominated for an Oscar.

This must have been a period where Nicholson wanted to escape into heavily made-up characters, based on the role he chose after completing *Hoffa*. Nicholson next accepted *Wolf* (1994). *Wolf* was based on the Wolf Man character that was most effectively performed by Lon Chaney Jr. in *The Wolf Man* (1941), part of the Universal horror film series. Although it grossed $130 million at the box office, *Wolf* was not a good movie and is hardly essential to the Jack Nicholson filmography. *Time Out* stated,

> Quite frankly, it's hard to fathom why exactly anyone would have wanted to make this slick, glossy, but utterly redundant werewolf movie. . . . Overall, this is needlessly polished nonsense: not awful; just toothless, gutless and bloodless.[1]

Nicholson then settled into an independent project for which his friend, actor Sean Penn, would be acting as auteur. Penn wrote the screenplay, was co-producing, and would also be directing *The Crossing Guard*.

THE CROSSING GUARD

(1995, Miramax)

★ ★ ★ ★

Director: Sean Penn
Screenplay: Sean Penn
Producers: Sean Penn, David Hamburger. *Cinematographer:* Vilmos Zsigmond.
    Editor: Jay Casidy
Cast: Jack Nicholson (Freddy Gale), David Morse (John Booth), Anjelica
    Huston (Mary), Robin Wright (Jojo), Piper Laurie (Helen Booth),
    Richard Bradford (Stuart Booth), Priscilla Barnes (Verna), David
    Baerwald (Peter), Robbie Robertson (Roger), John Savage (Bobby),
    Kari Wuhrer (Mia), Jennifer Leigh Warren (Jennifer), Kelita Smith
    (Tanya), Richard Sarafian (Sunny), Bobby Cooper (Coop), Jeff Morris
    (Silas), Buddy Anderson (Buddy), Edward L. Katz (Eddie), Joe Viterelli
    (Joe), Ry Ishibashi (Jeffrey), Leo Penn (Hank)
Released: November 16, 1995
Specs: 111 minutes; color
Availability: DVD (Echo Bridge)

A strong movie with well-drawn characters and some insightful direction, *The Crossing Guard* was a box office flop and is one of Jack Nicholson's least known movies. Despite the star power in front of and behind the camera, *The Crossing Guard* was independently produced and its distribution was more limited. Nicholson waived his usual fee. However, now that we can approach it as cinema, without regard to its lack of business success, it emerges as one of Nicholson's better performances from this period. It is not consistently well structured and its momentum is uneven, but *The Crossing Guard* remains an essential Jack Nicholson film because he is able to once again explore a truly complex character.

Nicholson plays Freddy Gale, a jewelry store owner whose daughter was, years earlier, struck by a drunk driver. The incident affected him emotionally at such an enormous level that it effectively destroyed his life. Once happy and successful, Freddy is now divorced from his wife, has no relationship with his other children, and spends his nights drinking, going to strip clubs, and soliciting prostitutes. Consumed by torment, he finally sees a possibility of closure when the drunk driver is released from prison after serving a five-year sentence. He goes to his ex-wife and announces that he plans to kill the man who was responsible for their daughter's death.

Nicholson plays Gale as very tense and low key but able to explode without warning. This is borne out when he visits his wife and her new husband at their home. He announces his intention to kill the drunk driver, prefacing by stating he has some "really great news." She tells him to leave the house, and he explodes with anger while she yells back, chastising him for obsessing over their daughter and ignoring that he has two other children.

The drunk driver is John Booth, whom we see leaving prison, being driven home by his delighted parents, and taking up residence in a fixed trailer on their property. Freddy sneaks into the trailer as Booth sleeps and fires at him, but he forgot to fill the magazine in the gun. Booth awakens, and the two discuss the situation. Booth understands Gale's obsession, and asks for a compromise. He asks to enjoy some freedom before Gale takes his life. Gale agrees to come back to kill him in three days. He is later shown angrily marking the days on his calendar at home.

Director Penn does an interesting method of presentation for each of these roles. Freddy Gale comes off as creepy, unpredictable, and volatile. Booth comes off as calm, remorseful, basically a good man who had a car accident where a child was killed. He is also tormented, but from another perspective. However, the man who committed the murder is not seen as the bad guy. The child's father is. It is a complex, fascinating look at those two characters.

Booth does what he can in three days, attempting to live his life and deal with his remorse. At one point he brings flowers to the child's grave, but leaves when he sees her mother there. Freddy, meanwhile, is jailed for starting a fight in a restaurant. While Booth develops a relationship with an attractive lady, Freddy continues to live in a morass of alcohol and strip joints. Both men are tormented, but only one of them is obsessed. Booth reveals to his lady that he was drunk and that it was purely an accident:

> I didn't know what happened. I just felt a bump. When I stopped I saw what happen. She was lying in the street all torn up. I could see her moving a little bit. When I got up to her I kind of knelt down. She apologized to me for not having looked both ways.

Gale, however, is tormented by a need for vengeance rather than consumed by guilt like Booth. He endures a nightmare that he tearfully explains to his ex-wife, where he comes to a crosswalk by their daughter's school and sees Booth is the crossing guard standing with a group of children, including their daughter. In the dream, he runs them all over.

Gale gets drunk and heads to Booth's trailer, but is stopped for drunk driving. He comes out of the car, his hands raised, and tells the officers there is a gun on the seat. He explains he has a permit, that he owns a jewelry store so the gun is for protection. As he is going through sobriety tests, he abruptly grabs his own gun and runs off before the officers can arrest him for drunk driving. To elude the police, he breaks into a home and finds himself in the bedroom of a little girl. He puts his finger to his lips to quiet her. When her father and the police enter her room, she says she is okay, guiding the police away. Gale thanks her and leaves the home.

Despite being older and in bad shape, Gale runs fast enough to elude two much younger and healthier police officers. Nicholson plays this effectively, wheezing audibly as he runs and being exhausted afterward, which reveals that his character is working from pure adrenaline. When he finally reaches the trailer, Booth is armed with a shotgun. Gale reveals the irony:

> I'll give you a laugh, kid. I got pulled over tonight by the police. The whole bit. You wanna guess what for? Drunk driving! I have a gun. I'm not particularly acquainted with the law, but I'm on the run, on your property, and I've got my gun. You can shoot me and get away clean. I'm gonna get my gun out of my pants here. I guess I'm gonna try and shoot you.

Booth drops his gun and runs. Gale pursues him. At one point he fires, but the wound is superficial. They end up in the cemetery where the daughter is buried. Booth says, "Your father's coming." Gale drops his gun and falls to the child's grave sobbing and apologizing. Booth takes Gale by the hand and they walk off as the sun starts to rise.

What is best about *The Crossing Guard* is Nicholson's performance. He stated in an interview with Roger Ebert that he took the job because of the role:

> This role was the other end of the pole from the Joker. It was a chance to get closer to first person acting: Less artifice, more interior, more behavior. The scenes didn't all consist of you servicing the plot. There was some air in there. This movie is almost naked. I don't have a limp or a lisp or a walk or a thing. In other words, I did this movie for the doing.[1]

Nicholson's character is unsettling and brutal, tense and angry, vengeful and uncompromising. Then, as the film progresses and the character evolves, he becomes more sympathetic, as we understand his torment more clearly. When he falls weeping at the grave alongside the man he is obsessed with killing, his torment has culminated. It's rare to see Nicholson play such vulnerable scenes, which makes those scenes where he breaks down in tears all the more powerful.

Actor Sean Penn wrote, directed, and co-produced this film, revealing his inspiration to *Interview* magazine:

> I didn't know what I wanted to write about that I could direct, and then Eric Clapton's child died—and it was such a wake-up call. I started writing *The Crossing Guard* the next day, and that just flowed. I knew that I wanted to write something for actors who'd be so good they'd really be able to tell me what the heart of the story was. I had a map in my head, which was going to tell me the story, but I also had the actors come in to rehearse scenes and what ideas they had that day.[2]

Not everything works here. Priscilla Barnes is unfortunately saddled with the thankless clichéd role of the proverbial stripper with a heart of gold who spends a portion of the film helping to anchor Gale's volatility. David Morse, as Booth, has a ham-handed soliloquy he slogs through as the killer tries to reveal his torment to his parents. Robin Wright, then Sean Penn's wife, is an attractive presence as the woman Booth connects with briefly, but the character never seems organic to the story.

Still, the film is filled with great scenes. Nicholson cascading into sobs as Gale tells his ex-wife over the phone about the nightmare he had is followed by a scene between Gale and his ex meeting at a diner in an attempt to sort out their respective torment and his obsession. When she reveals that she believes he's beyond her help, he lashes out and she leaves. Anjelica Huston, as the ex-wife, turns in one of the best performances in the film, remaining focused and strong like a woman who suffered tragedy but was somehow able to move on.

Critics were generally underwhelmed by the film but impressed by the performances. Janet Maslin stated in the *New York Times*,

> Mr. Nicholson lurches through this role with rekindled intensity, only occasionally (and in his climactic scene with Ms. Huston, quite scarily) summoning his trademark movie-star mannerisms. Though the particulars of Freddy's story aren't always believable, the fundamental nature of his ordeal comes through. Mr. Morse, who also appeared in "The Indian Runner," has the more achingly sensitive role, but he too captures the essential decency at the heart of Mr. Penn's screenplay. There aren't many stray ideas here, but the ones that *The Crossing Guard* tackles most earnestly are worth the attention.[3]

Kenneth Turan in the *Los Angeles Times* was far less impressed with Penn's work and even took some issue with the casting of Booth, while still praising Nicholson:

> Sean Penn brings the same visceral intensity and raw emotionality to writing and directing as he does to acting, and while that may sound like a good thing, it finally isn't. *The Crossing Guard*, Penn's second film behind the camera, is a troubling, troublesome movie whose makeshift structure cannot contain the powerful flood of passions that he and his cast have poured into it. . . . The way Booth is envisioned, capped by the casting of Morse, is also off. Though Morse is a capable actor, Booth is too much the gentle, saintly giant, too fine and sensitive a presence, to seem other than a hollow construct. And, fascinated by the possibilities of contrasting Freddy's boozing and wenching to Booth's philosophical discussions with sensitive artist Jojo (Robin Wright) about the nature of guilt, Penn has not noticed how schematic it all is. Looking convincingly bleary-eyed and believably self-destructive, Nicholson is as impressive as he's been in years as a man who has willfully turned his own life into hell on Earth.[4]

Barnes's role may be clichéd, but he pulls off the sensitive, soft performance that contrasts with Nicholson's very effectively.

After completing *The Crossing Guard*, Nicholson spent the following year doing three films that ranged from lackluster to being of interest on a cult level. *Blood and Wine* (1996) was a neo-noir made for $26 million, but grossed a little over $1 million at the box office. *Evening Star* (1996) was a tardy and misguided sequel to *Terms of Endearment* focusing on what became of the Shirley MacLaine character. Despite a cameo by Nicholson as a favor to MacLaine, *Evening Star* was savaged by critics and lost nearly $10 million at the box office. *Mars Attacks!* (1996) was Tim Burton's amusing takeoff on 1950s sci-fi movies, with Nicholson playing two roles. Despite its impressive intentions and the films by which it was inspired, *Mars Attacks!* is not a particularly good movie. It did later generate something of a cult following. Burton purposely wanted the special effects to be cheesy so they were reminiscent of '50s B movies, and Nicholson appears to have fun cheesing it up in both his roles. The movie further benefits from its large, amazing cast.

In 1997, Jack Nicholson, the actor who specializes in quirky roles, took on one of the quirkiest characters he'd ever had to portray. *As Good as It Gets* was not only a box office hit, but it garnered Nicholson another Best Actor Oscar.

AS GOOD AS IT GETS

(1997, TriStar Pictures)

★ ★ ★ ★ ★

Director: James L. Brooks
Screenplay: James L. Brooks, Mark Andrus, based on a story by Andrus
Producers: James L. Brooks, Bridget Johnson, Kristi Zea. *Cinematographer:*
    John Bailey. *Editor:* Richard Marks
Cast: Jack Nicholson (Melvin Udall); Helen Hunt (Carol); Greg Kinnear
    (Simon); Cuba Gooding Jr. (Frank); Skeet Ulrich (Vincent); Shirley
    Knight (Beverly); Yeardley Smith (Jackie); Lupe Ontiveros (Nora);
    Brian Doyle-Murray (Handyman); Patricia Childress, Rebekah Johnson,
    Missi Pyle, Leslie Stefanson, Tara Subkof (Waitresses); Jesse James
    (Spencer Connelly); Jamie Kennedy, Justin Herwick (Hustlers); Harold
    Ramis (Dr. Bettes); Danielle Spencer (Veterinarian); Lawrence Kasdan
    (Dr. Green); Julie Benz (Receptionist); Jimmy Workman (Sean); Linda
    Gehringer (Publisher)
Released: December 25, 1997
Specs: 139 minutes; Technicolor
Availability: DVD (Columbia TriStar)

In the opening scene of *As Good as It Gets*, Jack Nicholson's character puts a live little dog in the garbage chute, refers to a character played by Cuba Gooding Jr. as a "colored man," and insults a gay neighbor played by Greg Kinnear, calling him a "faggot." His only tentative affection seems to be toward Carol, played by Helen Hunt, a waitress at a diner. And somehow, Nicholson must make this character likable.

In the next few scenes, we realize Nicholson's character, Melvin Udall, has a myriad of special needs. He refuses to step on cracks as he walks down the street. He washes his hands with a new bar of soap, throws it away, and then opens a new bar to wash his face and disposes of that (his medicine cabinet is filled with newly wrapped soaps). He insists so passionately on sitting in "his booth" at a nearby diner that he insults a couple who happen to be there when he arrives. As his designated waitress, Carol, comes to take his order, he pulls plastic utensils out of a plastic bag.

Kinnear plays Simon, an artist who lives across the hall. Gooding is Frank, the art dealer who promotes Simon's work. Simon says to Udall, "You've never loved anything," and at the outset of the movie, this appears to be true. Udall is a writer who works from his apartment, has his set ways, deals with his obsessive-compulsive disorder, and simply wants to be left alone. When Simon knocks on Udall's door while he is writing, Udall comes to the door angrily and states,

> Never, never, interrupt me, okay? Not if there's a fire, not even if you hear the sound of a thud from my home and one week later there's a smell coming from there that can only be a decaying human body and you have to hold a hanky to your face because the stench is so thick that you think you're going to faint. Even then, don't come knocking. Or, if it's election night, and you're excited and you wanna celebrate because some fudgepacker that you date has been elected the first queer president of the United States and he's going to have you down to Camp David, and you want someone to share the moment with. Even then, don't knock. Not on this door. Not for *any* reason. Do you get me, sweetheart?

However, when Simon is brutally attacked by a hired male model and his friends, Frank strong-arms Udall into taking in Simon's dog while the artist recovers from his wounds. At this point, Udall's character evolves. He ends up responding favorably to the dog, and in the weeks Simon is recovering, Udall and the pet develop a bond. When Simon recovers and reclaims his dog, Udall weeps. The dog also acts forlorn and mopes about, missing the new master to whom he's given his allegiance.

Udall is one of the most complex characters Nicholson has played, even this late in his career. He is verbally abusive in so casual a manner that he doesn't even appear to realize who he might be offending. He needs his immediate world to be structured exactly as he deems necessary. When Carol is not at the restaurant, he calls her overweight replacement "elephant girl." When a fan of his books approaches him and asks, "How do you write women so well?" he quickly brushes her off with the insulting, "I think of a man and take away reason and accountability."

The level at which Udall is set in his ways is alternately fascinating and disturbing. When he goes to his restaurant and discovers that Carol is no longer working there, he insists they get her and allow him to pay her salary just to wait on him. When he leaves the restaurant under police insistence, the wait staff and customers applaud, having had enough of his abusive behavior.

Udall does good deeds for Carol. She has a child who is seriously ill, and her insurance has limited his medical care. Udall has money, as he is a best-selling author. His publisher's husband is a top-level pediatrician so he arranges to pay for the child's care from this top-level physician who Carol would otherwise never have been able to afford. The doctor tells Carol that her son "is going to feel a lot better from now on." While Carol tries to justify allowing this crazy person to help her out, we realize Udall's good gesture isn't altruism—he wants the child to get better so Carol can return to the restaurant and his schedule is not disrupted. Carol, concerned at the possibility of an ulterior motive, bluntly tells Udall she has no plans to sleep with him. He scoffs at the idea of that ever having been considered.

The evolution of the character is all about Nicholson's performance. While the script has the good deeds, Nicholson must expertly balance between these deeds and his character's underlying hostility toward others. When he finds that Simon's medical bills have caused him to go broke, Udall brings him soup and eventually agrees to drive him to his estranged parents' out-of-state home, so Simon can ask them for money. At the same time, when he sits in his booth at the restaurant with Frank and agrees to take Frank's car to drive Simon to his parents' home out of state, he tells Frank to leave because he doesn't like him. When Simon is sobbing over the fact that his art world friends have abandoned him in his time of need, Udall says, "You're a disgrace to depression." On top of this erratic wavering between good deeds and caustic behavior, Udall also has many positive aspects about his complex character. Not only is he a brilliant writer, but he has great taste in music, is a capable driver, and is a good dancer. His place is immaculately clean.

Nicholson explores the character's disorders along with his abilities. He talks Carol into joining him and Simon on the trip to his parents' house in Baltimore. They stay in a hotel. Simon has a lot on his mind and does not want to go out. So Carol and Udall go out alone. At one point he says, "This place makes me wear a jacket and tie and you get to wear a simple house dress." Carol is insulted and ready to leave.

Udall: I've got a really great compliment for you, and it's true.

Carol: I'm so afraid you're about to say something awful.

Udall: Don't be pessimistic, it's not your style. Okay, here I go: Clearly, a mistake. I've got this, what—ailment? My doctor, a shrink that I used to go to all the time, he says that in fifty or sixty percent of the cases, a pill really helps. I *hate* pills, very dangerous thing, pills. Hate. I'm using the word *hate* here, about pills. Hate. My compliment is, that night when you came over and told me that you would never . . . all right, well, you were there, you know what you said. Well, my compliment to you is, the next morning, I started taking the pills.

Carol: I don't quite get how that's a compliment for me.

Udall: You make me want to be a better man.

Carol: . . . That's maybe the best compliment of my life.

Udall: Well, maybe I overshot a little, because I was aiming at just enough to keep you from walking out.

Nicholson does a particularly brilliant job conveying his feelings while remaining cocky in tone. One can see by the look in his eye that he has strong feelings for Carol, but he is unable to stop himself from saying the wrong thing. The way he delivers the line "You make me want to be a better man" is just different enough from his usual tone to let us know he means it.

However, Udall is not used to friendly company with people, so he continues to say the wrong thing. He reveals to Carol that she should have sex with Simon in an attempt to perhaps make him heterosexual. When she storms out of the restaurant, Udall soon finds himself chatting with the bartender:

Well, it's not right to go into details, I got nervous. I screwed up, I said the wrong thing. Where if I hadn't, I could be in bed right now with a woman who, if you make her laugh, you got a life. Instead I'm here with you, a moron pushing the last legal drug.

Everything happens on the trip. Simon sketches Carol and has a revelation as an artist, and no longer wants to ask his parents for money. Udall falls in love with Carol, but doesn't know how to communicate with her. It gets to the point where upon returning home from the trip she tells Udall,

Nicholson in his third Oscar-winning performance (with Greg Kinnear) in *As Good as It Gets*. *Columbia / TriStar / Photofest* © *Columbia / TriStar*

"I don't care what you did for me, I don't think I want to know you anymore. All you do is make me feel bad about myself."

Udall becomes so fond of Simon that when they discover the penniless artist's apartment has been sublet, Udall invites Simon to live with him. "I had them bring your things and put them in this room. I never use it." Simon tells Udall he loves him. Udall responds, "You know, kid, I'd be the luckiest guy in the world if that did it for me."

Carol feels remorse for what she said to Udall and calls to apologize. In this scene, Carol points out all of the complexities of Udall's character. She states that she cares about him and recognizes his great qualities, but can't handle his inability to communicate with her: "You're not ready, and you're too old to not be ready." Udall realizes he is in love with Carol and tells Simon, "She's evicted me from my life." Simon responds, "Was it really all that great?" As Udall prepares to go see Carol, he realizes he did not lock the door when he arrived home. One of his compulsions was naturally ignored.

When he arrives at Carol's home, she says, "Come in and try not to ruin everything by being you." He responds, "Maybe we can live without the wise cracks," forcing her to realize something about herself. Finally, Udall uses his command of the English language to tell Carol how he truly feels:

> I might be the only person on the face of the earth that knows you're the greatest woman on earth. I might be the only one who appreciates how amazing you are in every single thing that you do, and how you are with Spencer, "Spence," and in every single thought that you have, and how you say what you mean, and how you almost always mean something that's all about being straight and good. I think most people miss that about you, and I watch them, wondering how they can watch you bring their food, and clear their tables and never get that they just met the greatest woman alive. And the fact that I get it makes me feel good, about me.

As Good as It Gets has strong individual scenes, snappy dialogue, and brilliant performances. Nicholson has an opportunity to investigate several layers of a very enigmatic character and he makes the most of it. He fidgets, rubs his hands together, and never appears to be completely still. Even when relaxed and in conversation, his eyes dart and squint, his brow furls and unfurls, his head weaves, and his body slightly sways. It is a truly remarkable performance. The film's only flaw is that it tends to lapse into sentimentality in some of its serious scenes. But that's a trifling quibble. There isn't a structured plot to the film; it revolves around what is happening in the characters' lives at the moment, making the performances all the more crucial. And each of the three main characters have their own personal issues. And although the characters have very different problems, they are able to help each other overcome them. Every actor offers some of their career-best work, but Nicholson really delivers on what is probably his most complex character in a career filled with complex characters. On the one hand he gets to play his trademark curmudgeon, but the sweet little gestures he makes throughout the film make you love him, even when on the surface there's nothing to love about him.

In a review for the *Washington Post*, Desson Howe stated,

> Melvin is an obsessive-compulsive SOB, Simon's recovering from a severe beating, and Carol's son could die from asthma at any moment. And this is a comedy? For Brooks, life is only parenthetically about suffering. What matters to him—and what usually entertains us—is the way his characters complain, behave and verbalize as they undergo this lifelong misery at work, in the family, or in their fractured relationships. Brooks is helped immeasurably by his performers. No one plays the beast cuter than Nicholson. . . . He turns nastiness into some kind of malignant charm.[1]

Nicholson was pleased to once again be working with writer-director James L. Brooks, who had directed him to a Best Actor Oscar for *Terms of Endearment*. As it turned out, Nicholson also won that Oscar for his performance in *As Good as It Gets*, as did Helen Hunt for Best Actress. Both also won Golden Globe awards, while other Oscar nominations included Greg Kinnear for Best Supporting Actor, as well as Best Original Score, Best Original Screenplay, Best Editing, and Best Picture. While it lost those, the film did win the Golden Glove for Best Film—Musical or Comedy.

As Good as It Gets was budgeted at $50 million, but it was a very big hit at the box office, grossing over $300 million. It was the third-highest-grossing film of 1997 after *Titanic* and the James Bond feature *Tomorrow Never Dies*. It is the second-highest-grossing Jack Nicholson film after *Batman*.

For his next film, Jack Nicholson once again agreed to work in a Sean Penn–directed film. However, this time, the movie would be a major studio production, with a $35 million budget, not an indie like *The Crossing Guard*. Jack expected his usual fee.

26

THE PLEDGE

(2001, Warner Bros.)

★ ★ ★

Director: Sean Penn
Screenplay: Jerzy Kromolowski, Mary Olson-Kromolowski, based on the
    book by Friedrich Dürrenmatt
Producers: Sean Penn, Michael Fitzgerald, Elie Samaha. *Cinematographer:* Chris
    Menges. *Editor:* Jay Cassidy
Cast: Jack Nicholson (Jerry Black), Patricia Clarkson (Margaret Larsen),
    Benicio Del Toro (Toby Jay Wadenah), Robin Wright Penn (Lori),
    Aaron Eckhart (Stan), Helen Mirren (Doctor), Michael O'Keefe
    (Duane), Tom Noonan (Gary), Vanessa Redgrave (Annalise), Mickey
    Rourke (Olstad), Sam Shephard (Eric), Harry Dean Stanton (Floyd),
    Lois Smith (Helen), Beau Daniels (Rudy), Dale Dickey (Strom), Pauline
    Roberts (Chrissy), Taryn Knowles (Ginny)
Released: January 19, 2001
Specs: 124 minutes; color
Availability: DVD (Warner Home Video)

Sean Penn directs Jack Nicholson in another film that deals with the tragic
loss of a child and the central character's obsession. Except *The Pledge* is
not as good of a movie as *The Crossing Guard* had been.

Nicholson plays Jerry Black, a detective about to retire who is thrown
a surprise retirement party and given a fishing trip as a gift. The party is

interrupted by reports that a murdered child has been discovered in the woods. Jerry goes with his fellow detectives to the case, elects to inform the parents, and swears on his soul that he will find her killer. A mentally deficient Native American man is considered a suspect and despite his limited communication skills, appears to confess to the crime. When he grabs an officer's gun and kills himself, the detectives believe the case is closed. But Jerry is not convinced this man was the killer.

Nicholson plays Jerry with his classic brand of stoicism, and Penn understands how to properly frame his movie's star performance. The scene where Jerry comes to deliver the tragic news to the child's parents shows them as workers on a turkey farm, in an enclosure filled with the birds, which Nicholson stoically wades through in a medium tracking shot as he approaches the parents. His telling them the news is not done with dialogue. Penn frames this in a long shot and shows the reaction purely through the physical reaction of the parents. It is a nicely crafted scene that offers an impressive vision on the part of the filmmaker.

Jerry's obsession is different than the character he had played in *The Crossing Guard*. In the previous film, his character has a personal stake in the tragedy as it is his own daughter who is killed by a drunk driver, thus upsetting his life forever. In *The Pledge*, his personal stake is his word.

Rather than go on his fishing trip, Jerry instead continues to investigate a crime the other detectives believe is solved. He questions the grandmother, the child's best friend; he looks at her crayon art and notices a pattern that he believes might be a clue. He asks that the case be reopened. He is refused. But his friend Stan at the detective bureau runs data through the system that gives Jerry more information about similar crimes, which assists in his further investigation.

It is at this point that *The Pledge* loses focus. When Jerry connects with a mother and her young child, getting involved with their lives and offering support, the film loses focus and meanders onto tangential stories involving the mother, her abusive ex, and their daily lives. There is an attempt to maintain some level of tension because the child is about the same age as the murdered girl and soon befriends a local minister of whom Jerry is suspicious, but these scenes do not maintain the consistent level of suspense and intrigue as the earlier ones. The film shifts gears once the child says she "met the wizard today," and there are clues that connect to the murder Jerry is still trying to solve. Having a girl present the same age as the girl who was murdered seems to give Jerry a more concrete reason to catch the killer; otherwise, it feels like a rather strange obsession to have, as he didn't have any personal relationship with the murdered girl or her family.

It is interesting how Penn brackets the narrative with Jerry sitting outside a gas station mumbling to himself. This occurs first at the outset of the movie, the ensuing narrative being told in flashback. It happens again at the end, indicating Jerry remains unconvinced that the killer isn't still at large and that he reneged on his pledge to the murdered girl's parents.

What makes *The Pledge* essential to the Jack Nicholson filmography is his concentrated performance as Jerry. While the Melvin Udall character in *As Good as It Gets* is quite complex, Jerry is devoid of complexities. He is a very straightforward character who is obsessed with solving the crime he believes remains unsolved, despite conventional wisdom. He is focused, on note, only being distracted by the separate world of the mother and her child in a tangent that offsets the evenness of the film. Nicholson's performance as Jerry also shows a larger transition in the actor's career. With Jerry and other characters, he does not try to ignore the aging process, allowing himself to play characters who are older, disaffected, retired, but never completely settled. They never seem to give up hope, even when the odds seem to be against their success.

Nicholson stated in an interview with Cinema.com,

> It was a very dark character and I find it easy to identify with that. There's a sense of hopelessness and absurdity to his life and those are philosophical kinds of issues that have always been very close to my heart. Not that I take such a dim view of the world, but I understand those feelings and moods and it wasn't hard for me to throw myself into his world. That's why he's so desperate and driven to solve the murder. It's his way of fighting back against all the shit in the world and all the meaninglessness out there. He's trying to find some purpose and vindication in a life that's become a black hole.[1]

The Pledge was Jack Nicholson's first film in four years. He told Cinema .com in an interview,

> The only decision I made was that after *As Good as It Gets* I wanted to travel a bit and not think about work for a year. I gave myself a kind of year-long bonus to just relax and stay clear from all the phone calls and meetings and other garbage that's part of being in this business. But then I started getting involved in a lot of projects and I wasn't that happy with a lot of the scripts I was getting and a few films simply never got off the ground because of financing or other problems. We were supposed to make *The Pledge* at least a year before we actually shot it, so that was another delay because the money wasn't in place. I certainly never planned on that happening, but it's OK. At this point in my life, I'd rather wait for one good project than just rush ahead and take what comes.[2]

The Pledge was made for $35 million and grossed less than $30 million, failing to make back its production costs. While this is better than the independently produced *The Crossing Guard*, the previous film was more focused and consistent. However, *The Pledge* does show Jack Nicholson effectively continuing to transition into older roles. It was a transition he would continue for the remainder of his film career, even exploring areas of aging that had not been a part of any previous character.

Critics were rather pleased with *The Pledge* and noted the Penn-Nicholson cohesion, despite the movie's lack of box office success. Stephen Holden stated in the *New York Times*,

> The force with which Mr. Nicholson evokes the volatile, frightening place where male rage, fear, grief, loneliness and a warped sense of honor converge and explode suggests that he really is Mr. Penn's soul mate.[3]

Jack Nicholson would not wait four years to make another movie. In fact, the following year, he once again offered one of his finest performances and continued to embrace the aging process. As he grows old with his characters while retaining a youthful vitality in his regular life, Jack Nicholson was able to explore several different perspectives on aging. With his next film, he mined this concept far more deeply than any other film, and the results were quite remarkable.

ABOUT SCHMIDT

(2003, New Line Cinema)

★ ★ ★ ★

Director: Alexander Payne
Screenplay: Alexander Payne, Jim Taylor, based on the novel by Louis Begley
Producers: Michael Besman, Harry Gittes. *Cinematographer:* James Glennon.
   Editor: Kevin Tent
Cast: Jack Nicholson (Warren Schmidt), Kathy Bates (Roberta Hertzel),
   Hope Davis (Jeannie Schmidt), Dermot Mulroney (Randall Hertzel),
   June Squibb (Helen Schmidt), Howard Hessman (Larry Hertzel),
   Harry Groener (John Rusk), Connie Ray (Vicki Rusk), Len Cariou
   (Ray Nichols), Mark Venhuizen (Duncan Hertzel), Cherly Hamada
   (Saundra), Matt Winston (Gary Nordin)
Released: January 3, 2003
Specs: 125 minutes; color
Availability: DVD (New Line)

It appears that during this point in his career, Jack Nicholson was reinventing himself with every performance. Once the maverick outsider who challenged authority and the norm, Nicholson was now old enough to play a fading relic of the establishment. It is yet another one of the finest performances of his long career.

Warren Schmidt is a hardworking insurance man who is retiring, but soon discovers he is unable to adjust to being retired. Warren is one of those men whose entire life was consumed and defined by his career, and without it, he seems lost. Looking for a purpose, he sponsors an overseas foster child, using the idea of another person far from his immediate world as a sounding board for a series of random letters. It is the only outlet where Schmidt can reveal his true feelings about everything. This idea provides a nice framing device for each sequence of the film.

We immediately sense Warren's feeling of alienation and loneliness at a retirement dinner in the opening scene. He listens, stone-faced, to testimonials from his peers, then chooses to sit alone at the bar, ordering a drink and not appearing to want to socialize with anyone or celebrate anything. Nicholson maintains that element of the character as he and his wife plan to see the world in a giant Winnebago. His wife exhibits enthusiasm for their plans, but Schmidt remains grounded and unaffected.

Through his letters, by which we're informed through a voiceover, he reveals that he was unhappy with his job, has grown weary of his wife ("Who's this old lady sleeping in my bed?"), and can no longer connect effectively with his daughter. He attempts to reach out to the young executive who replaced him and is not only dismissed as not being needed, but as he leaves the building he sees that remnants of his former office have been discarded as trash. When his wife dies suddenly, he has to deal with another type of loss, and yet another readjustment. His daughter confronts him for not spending enough on the casket; she and her fiancé, Randall, recommend shallow books about coping; and her fiancé tries to get Schmidt to invest in a shady business scheme.

It is this adjustment period that is most revealing about the character. Schmidt tells all to his foster child in another letter that is revealed to us with a voiceover. Meanwhile, we see that he has reached the very depths of loneliness, not even bothering to get dressed when he goes grocery shopping. He just throws a coat over his pajamas and buys precooked frozen dinners, buying weeks' and weeks' worth to maintain his isolated existence. His house is unkempt, flies are starting to appear around the pile of unwashed dishes, and Schmidt wanders about from room to room. His letters to the foster child are his only connection to the outside world.

Realizing he does indeed miss his wife, despite having grown tired of her toward the end, Schmidt wanders in her closet to feel closer to her. He stumbles upon a box of love letters that show she had been having an affair with their good friend Ray. Angered, he hastily boxes up her clothing and tosses them at a used clothing store. He then stakes out the barber shop where Ray works and confronts him about the affair. Schmidt's entire life—

career, marriage, and fatherhood—now seem like they were for naught. He decides to simply get into his massive Winnebago and travel alone.

Schmidt's situation continues to be more and more isolated and unhappy as the film progresses. He plans to come out to see his daughter, whose reaction clearly communicates that she doesn't like the idea. He visits his childhood home, now occupied by a computer store. He wanders around his old college campus, even eating in the cafeteria with members of what was once his fraternity, but he is responded to with disaffected politeness at best. When Schmidt parks his Winnebago at a campsite, other mobile home campers stop in to visit him, want to see inside his large vehicle, invite him to dinner, and so on. Schmidt doesn't relate to these people any more than he has the others. After a few beers and looking at a boring photo album, he makes a pass at the wife while the husband goes out for more beer, thus ending the evening rather abruptly. He drives away in his Winnebago, separating himself from the situation—something he cannot always do. However, this incident causes him to understand the situation between Ray and his wife. He calls Ray and leaves a message that he is willing to talk over the affair. He sits on a rooftop speaking to the stars and offering understanding to his wife. He determines that a shooting star is a message that she understands too.

Dermot Mulroney, Hope Davis, and Nicholson in *About Schmidt*. *New Line Cinema / Photofest*
© *New Line Cinema*

When Schmidt spends a few days at the home of Randall's mother, he sees arguments, dysfunction, and behaviors that show his isolated existence to actually be preferable. He begs his daughter in a private conversation not to marry into this family. He explains a nightmare he had:

> The other night I had a dream and it was very real. Your mother was there and you were there and your aunt Estelle. And there was a . . . well, it wasn't really a spaceship, it was more like a blimp or an orb of some kind. And then a bunch of weird creatures came out and started trying to take you away, and you wanna know what? They all looked like Randall. Do you understand? And I was jumping up and down to save you.

She dismisses him by saying, "You're just wigging out a little and mom is not here to calm you down." She concludes the conversation by stating, "Okay, you listen to me. I am getting married the day after tomorrow and you are going to come to my wedding and you are going to sit there and enjoy it and support me or else you can just turn right around right now and go back to Omaha."

Schmidt is unable to sleep comfortably on the waterbed at Randall's mother's house. The next day his back is in such bad shape that there is some concern he might miss the wedding. The mother feeds him soup, telling him about the sex life of her past marriages, of his daughter and her son, and her own reaction to sex ("I had my first orgasm when I was six—in ballet class."). Eventually, she suggests he soak in her hot tub. However, when she comes into the room naked, joins him, and makes a pass, he flees her home. At the wedding, despite his continued misgivings that are essentially proved by Randall's boorish behavior, Schmidt gives a toast that is heartfelt and supportive while still being a bit rambling.

The film concludes as Schmidt returns home and a voiceover indicates his most recent letter to his foster child:

> Relatively soon, I will die. Maybe in twenty years, maybe tomorrow, it doesn't matter. Once I am dead and everyone who knew me dies too, it will be as though I never existed. What difference has my life made to anyone. None that I can think of. None at all.

He has resigned himself to being of no real consequence, until he finds in his mail a pile of letters that have accumulated while he was gone. They are all of his letters to his foster child, accompanied by a note that explains that the child cannot read a word of English. A drawing the child drew of a tall stick figure holding hands with a smaller one brings Schmidt to tears as the film ends.

About Schmidt allows Jack Nicholson to play an old man who truly is old, not one who has a wily sensibility and some youthful vitality. He plays a lonely man who truly is lonely, not isolated with an underlying intention or obsessions. His stoicism is not borne of military training or hard-fought accomplishment. He is not brimming with charisma, controlling his situations, or confronting his demons. He is simply going about his way, searching for some meaning of his existence, attempting to find some level of even the most marginal accomplishment. The drawing from the foster child makes him weep because he realizes he has finally made a genuine, positive impact on another's life.

Filmmaker Alexander Payne originally included a scene in the film that was an homage to the iconic restaurant encounter from *Five Easy Pieces*. However, in this one, Nicholson's character responds to the waitress by cowering and agreeing with her rather than standing up to her and insisting on his special order being filled. The preview audiences reportedly loved the scene, but Payne felt that because it called attention to Nicholson the actor's other work, it took the viewer out of the context of the film. He's probably right, but one can argue that it would also show how Schmidt's agreeable complacency was the polar opposite of the rebellious attitude exhibited in the earlier film.

Critics were impressed with, as well as intrigued by, Nicholson's work on this film. In a review for *New York* magazine, critic Peter Rainer stated,

> Jack Nicholson is not being "Jack" in this film, and for some people, that's reason enough to croon Oscar carols. But his work here, in its own impacted way, is just as outlandish as in his trademark performances. Nicholson is a master at playing to an audience, and he gives Warren the rigid composure of a straitlaced man who, deep down, exudes a faint daffiness. We keep searching his face for the little tics and quivers that tell us something is pulsing beneath the blandness. Warren is supposed to be reclaiming lost opportunities, he's supposed to be at a crossroads; but what we see, perhaps intentionally, is a man who never had much to lose.[1]

Nicholson himself explained his concept, as well as his approach, to the character of Warren Schmidt in an interview for the *Guardian*:

> What I have always done is not necessarily have to act but become the physicality of the person. For Schmidt I thought, what would I have been like if I had lived this sedentary kind of life. And I got into it enough to where I really

didn't like it. I thought, am I ever going to be able to return to my regular self?[2]

About Schmidt proved that there was a place in motion pictures for an older Jack Nicholson. This young rebel of *Five Easy Pieces* was still relevant some thirty years later. He received an Oscar nomination for his role as Schmidt, which he did not win. He did win a Golden Globe for Best Actor in a Motion Picture Drama. Upon accepting the award, Nicholson quipped, "I'm a little surprised. I thought we made a comedy."

It is rather surprising that *About Schmidt* is widely classified as a comedy, because outside of a few humorous scenes it's really one of the most depressing movies of Nicholson's career. Even though the final scene could be considered mildly uplifting, it's just a sad, sad story. However, it is remarkable to see Nicholson excel at playing a character who is so opposite to the kind he usually plays. Usually his roles are people who are aggressive; they see the need to do something and they go do it, not just in movies like *One Flew over the Cuckoo's Nest,* but even in more recent movies like *The Crossing Guard* and *The Pledge.* Schmidt is so passive; even his attempts to confront Ray about the affair with his wife and to convince his daughter not to get married don't amount to anything.

About Schmidt was made for $30 million and grossed over $100 million at the box office. However, Nicholson felt he needed something of a respite from having played such a heavy and demanding role in what he had perceived as a comedy and what many critics and moviegoers saw as a more serious film. There would be no confusion as to whether Jack Nicholson's next film was a comedy. It starred comedian Adam Sandler.

ANGER MANAGEMENT

(2003, Columbia)

★★ ½

Director: Peter Segal
Screenplay: David Dorfman
Producers: Barry Bernardi, Jack Giarraputo. *Cinematographer:* Donald
     McAlpine. *Editor:* Jeff Gourson
Cast: Adam Sandler (Dave Buznik); Jack Nicholson (Dr. Buddy Rydell); Marisa
     Tomei (Linda); Luis Guzmán (Lou); Allen Covert (Andrew); Lynne
     Thigpen (Judge); Kurt Fuller (Frank); Johnathan Lourghran (Nate);
     Krista Allen (Stacy); January Jones (Gina); Woody Harrelson (Galaxia/
     Gary); John Turturro (Chuck); Kevin Nealon (Sam); Conrad Goode
     (Bailiff/Lexus Man); John McEnroe, Rudy Giuliani, Derek Jeter, Roger
     Clemens (Themselves); Heather Graham (Kendra); John C. Reilly
     (Arnie Shankman—Older); Brent Tarnol (Arnie Shankman—Younger);
     Nils Allen Stewart (Tiny); Harry Dean Stanton (Blind Man)
Released: April 11, 2003
Specs: 106 minutes; color
Availability: DVD (Sony)

By the time of *Anger Management*, comedian Adam Sandler had extended
past his success as a cast member of TV's *Saturday Night Live* and starred
in a series of hit comedy features. Films like *Billy Madison* (1995), *Happy
Gilmore* (1996), *The Wedding Singer* (1998), *The Waterboy* (1998), and *Big
Daddy* (1999) allowed Sandler to create a well-liked character in popular

movies. He wrote or co-wrote many of his films. Their box office success was such that he was able to form his own production company, film a movie like *Anger Management* with a cast of recognizable film veterans, and arrange for Jack Nicholson to be his co-star.

Nicholson's most recent comedy at this level of boorishness was *Goin' South*, which he also directed. That film had been made twenty-five years earlier, so *Anger Management* is another example of Nicholson pursuing roles that are very different from one another. The quirky elements of his screen persona lend themselves well to this sort of comedy, so the idea of Jack Nicholson playing a most outrageous, unorthodox therapist who works with Sandler's character—an unassuming, mild-mannered man who gets railroaded into anger management classes due to a series of misunderstandings—has great potential. Unfortunately, it is mostly unrealized.

Sandler is Dave Buznik, whose entire personality is informed by a humiliating incident where a bully pulls down his pants just as he is about to get his first kiss. Dave is now withdrawn, cowardly, and mildly agreeable. However, during a business flight when he is seated next to Dr. Buddy Rydell, his life is disrupted and he becomes redefined as something he could never be. Trying to sleep, Dave is constantly awakened by Rydell's raucous laughter at a silly in-flight movie. He decides to give up trying to nap and decides to watch the movie. He asks for a headset; the stewardess ignores his request and keeps talking to her friend. As she passes Dave, he gently touches her arm and politely asks again for his headset. She responds as if assaulted, accuses him of raising his voice, and calls security, and Dave eventually finds himself in court. He is found guilty and sentenced to anger management therapy. He finds Rydell's practice and asks the doctor to sign papers indicating he does not need anger management. He is asked to attend one session.

Sandler is adept at playing either a boisterous, obnoxious individual or a mild, unassuming Everyman victim, two basic comedy characters. In fact, since he usually plays volatile characters who are quick to anger, his character in this movie is a joke in and of itself. Nicholson happily dives into idiosyncratic characters with great flourish. So both actors are confidently working within parameters that each finds comfortable as well as challenging. Sandler can withdraw into his character with tentative verbal delivery and stammering confusion, while Nicholson can explode with the edgiest improvisations.

David Dorfman's screenplay draws each character well, leaving opportunities for both actors to explore their respective ideas for their roles. Interestingly, and adding to the comic sensibility, Dorfman has the most wrongheaded ideas be successful while that which is considered correct consistently fails. Dave simply making a polite request develops into his being uncharacteristically branded as dangerously angry, while those who exhibit disruptive behavior are responded to in a positive manner. Adam Sandler recalled in an interview:

> We worked very hard on that script with Jack (Nicholson). We just made sure we liked every line in the movie. Then when we got on the set and we're rehearsing the scene and it's working, you try and come up with things on the fly, sure. I laughed my ass off at every take where Nicholson takes his plate of eggs and throws it against the wall! I enjoyed hearing him scream: "I said over easy!" I don't know why that made me laugh but I couldn't hold in my laughter.[1]

Dave is assigned to connect completely with Rydell, so they must remain inseparable, sleeping in the same bed, traveling together, and never being out of one another's sight. Some of the film's highlights include Dave confronting his old bully nemesis, now a monk in a monastery, and tormenting him in the same childish manner as he'd been bullied twenty-five years earlier as Rydell holds off all the other monks with a gun that turns out to be a water pistol. During a therapy session, the other patients include John McEnroe, who revisits an old tennis outburst with Nicholson. Rydell calms Dave by having the two of them sing songs from *West Side Story* while their parked car holds up traffic. When Dave finally becomes a more aggressive character, he takes over a ball game at Yankee Stadium and proclaims his love for his girlfriend, Linda, who had, over the course of the narrative, become involved with Rydell. However, this leads to a conclusion that seems bit sentimental and even rather predictable (all of the conflicts that led up to the climax were part of his "treatment").

The film is uneven, with outrageous comedy trading with mechanical slapstick, and ranging wildly from funny moments to eye-rolling misfires. But in a study of Jack Nicholson's work, it is fascinating to see him gleefully playing Dr. Rydell by embracing every quirky behavior in Dorfman's script, and likely adding some of his own. Nicholson liked playing characters as different from the previous one as possible, and Rydell is indeed as different from Schmidt as one can imagine. Critic Roger Ebert stated,

> Nicholson's early scenes are his best, because he brings an intrinsic interest to every character he plays. He wears a beard and works his eyebrows and sardonic grin with the zeal of a man who was denied them during the making of *About Schmidt*.[2]

However, the good performances, interesting concept, and various high-lights are not enough to overcome the unevenness, lapses into sentiment, and generally poor structure of the film. Elvis Mitchell wrote in the *New York Times*,

> Mr. Sandler and Mr. Nicholson are two defensive talents, and it's Mr. Nichol-son who finally buckles, swept onto the wave of indifference that is often the chief ingredient in Sandler vehicles. That standard flatness probably made Pe-ter Segal an apt director for "Management." In the list of adjectives that one could append to Mr. Segal, the word slick is not one of them — that capacity seems beyond his means. Some of the movie is so primitively staged that you can almost hear someone leafing through the book of instructions that came with the camera.[3]

While it is by no means among Jack Nicholson's best movies (or even one of Sandler's better efforts), Nicholson approaches the role with such abandon that he is a delight to watch. Because of the talent involved, *Anger Management* had a budget of $75 million, but it grossed nearly $200 million. Adam Sandler movies were quite popular at the time, while Jack Nicholson added further box office insurance. Interestingly, Jack Nicholson was not Sandler's first choice. He originally wanted Eddie Murphy for the role, who turned it down. Murphy's approach to the character would likely have made *Anger Management* a much different movie.

Jack Nicholson actually steals all of the scenes from Sandler—Sandler's character is almost too bland in comparison. Without Nicholson, this would be even less of a film than it already is. As it is, it is a mildly amusing com-edy punctuated by a few funny moments, but most of the humor is juvenile and the story itself rather pointless. The fact that it is so predictable makes sitting through those not-so-great scenes even worse.

When the film was released, Adam Sandler gave free copies to US military bases in the Persian Gulf. These versions included a five-minute introduction by Sandler personally thanking the troops for their service. A television series based on the movie premiered in June 2012 with Charlie Sheen in the role originated by Jack Nicholson.

SOMETHING'S GOTTA GIVE

(2003, Columbia)

★ ★

Director: Nancy Meyers
Screenplay: Nancy Meyers
Producers: Nancy Meyers, Bruce A. Block. *Cinematographer:* Michael Balhaus.
    Editor: Joe Hutshing
Cast: Jack Nicholson (Harry Sanborn); Diane Keaton (Erica Barry); Keanu
    Reeves (Julian Mercer); Frances McDormand (Zoe); Amanda Peet
    (Marin); Jon Favreau (Leo); Paul Michael Glaser (Dave); Rachel Ticotin
    (Dr. Martinez); Paige Butcher, Tanya Sweet, Kristine Szabo, Daniella
    Van Graas, Tamara Spoelder, Sonja Francis, Vanessa Trump, Kathy
    Tong (Beauties); Melette Le Blanc-Cabot, Suzanne Dizon, Audrey
    Wasilewski, Roxanne Beckgord, Robin Pearson Rose (Nurses);
    Michelle Fabiano, Catherine McGoohan, Blaine Allen, Julia Rose, Joan
    Adelle Nelson, Cindy Joseph, Alexandra Neil, Susan Misner (Harry's
    Old Girlfriends)
Released: December 12, 2003
Specs: 128 minutes; color
Availability: DVD (Sony)

Continuing to take on diverse roles, Jack Nicholson went from a boorish
Adam Sandler comedy to this lightweight romantic comedy from Nancy
Meyers. *Something's Gotta Give* is a very average movie, not much of a
vehicle for Nicholson to explore his comic sensibilities.

The film confronts May–December romances from a couple of different perspectives. Nicholson is Harry Sanborn, a wealthy, successful record label owner whose company specializes in popular hip-hop recordings. His occupation allows him the attitude that, despite his age, he has a tangible connection to youthfulness. He is dating Marin, a twenty-nine-year-old auctioneer whose mother, Erica, a playwright, works hard to accept their relationship. Harry suffers a heart attack while fooling around with Marin, and he is quickly rushed to the hospital, where his young doctor exhibits an attraction to Erica. The doctor states that Harry should stay nearby so his progress can be monitored. Arrangements are made for him to stay at Erica's home. This causes the usual complications, especially when Harry accidentally walks into Erica's room and sees her naked.

This first portion of *Something's Gotta Give* examines the May–December relationships from different perspectives. First, we look at Harry's attitude toward his own youthful prowess despite being much older than Marin. They seem very lopsided, very incongruous. We understand why Harry is attracted to Marin, but we are not quite sure what she sees in this much older man. She does not appear to be so shallow that she'd be attracted to his wealth and success. Harry's concept of his own youthfulness is challenged when some simple dilly-dallying in the bedroom results in a heart attack.

The doctor being attracted to Erica is another perspective. While tending to Harry in a calm, professional manner, his attraction to the much older woman is quite obvious. Erica is more grounded and sensible than Harry, so her reaction is as much embarrassment as it is being flattered.

Erica and Harry being forced to spend time under the same roof causes them to eventually develop an attraction to each other. Harry amicably parts with Marin and spends more time with Erica. Eventually, he is well enough to return to his own life and move out of Erica's house. Erica has maintained a friendship with her ex-husband (Marin's father), and attends a dinner party with him and his new fiancée, mostly because Marin is having a hard time dealing with her father's impending remarriage. Erica, however, is supportive of her ex's engagement. While in the restaurant, Erica sees Harry with another woman, confronts him, and then flees. Harry suffers chest pains and believes it to be another heart attack, but after examination, it turns out to simply be stress.

It is here where the film's narrative structure falls flat. There is the sitcom-level humor that permeates the rather predictable attraction between Harry and Erica. There is Marin's complete acceptance of Harry no longer wanting her and instead wanting her mother. Finally, the story reveals that Marin's entire attraction to Harry was likely due to filial issues (based on her reaction to her father's impending marriage). It is a combination of lazy convenience and uneven plot points.

Erica's seeing Harry with the other woman leads to a hurt Erica deciding to emotionally heal by writing a play about the experience. It's a hit. This gives Harry yet another panic attack. Months later, Harry finds out from Marin that Erica is celebrating her birthday in Paris. Harry flies to her, but discovers she is there with the young doctor, whom she has been dating. Harry later finds himself looking over the river Seine, feeling melancholy, until Erica shows up in a taxi stating she realizes she belongs with Harry. A closing epilogue show them with Marin and her new husband, all getting along nicely.

Stating that the film has "the most painfully contrived premise since the cancellation of *Three's Company*," Christopher Orr of the *Atlantic* also stated,

> Meyer's authorial laziness is further enabled by the casting of Keaton and Nicholson, both of whom are so familiar to moviegoers that the business of developing their characters is largely done for her. Nicholson is playing Nicholson, right down to the sunglasses and cigars, in the most self-parodying role of a career characterized by self-parody. Indeed, the only way a man this coarse and fat and vain could get hot young sex in his sixties is if he actually is Jack Nicholson; if we for one moment believed that this lout was really a record producer named Harry Sanborn, the character would immediately be rendered either absurd or repulsive. (If you saw a 67-year-old man leer ostentatiously at a young woman's bottom in the grocery store and proceed to simulate oral sex on his ice cream cone, would you find it playfully charming or merely grotesque?) And Keaton is playing Keaton: She still makes do with her ostentatious collection of tics and gestures that will be familiar to anyone who's followed her work, especially her 1970s collaborations with Woody Allen. She stutters and giggles, she flips her hair and bites her lip, perennially caught between bubbly enthusiasm and gnawing self-doubt.[1]

It is interesting how the film wavers between understanding the situations presented by the narrative and being offended and unsettled by them. Erica is mature enough to accept Marin's relationship with Harry, but isn't completely comfortable with being courted by the much younger doctor. When Marin detects sparks developing between her mother and Harry, she breaks up with Harry quite amicably, saying to her mother, "He's all yours." However, she has trouble accepting her father remarrying. Finally, Erica confronts Harry when he is with another woman despite their never having made a true commitment to each other.

There is nothing sharp or witty about this romantic comedy, and it is only diverting because actors like Nicholson, Diane Keaton (as Erica), and Amanda Peet (as Marin) make it that way. The situations are pat, predictable, and only amusing at a most superficial level. A scene like Erica insisting they take Harry's blood pressure during foreplay, before they consummate their relationship, is what this film considers a comic highlight.

Jack Nicholson was pleased to be reunited with Diane Keaton, whom he'd worked with in *Reds* decades earlier. He told Rebecca Murray for About.com,

> I've always had tremendous affection for Keaton. I think so does everyone else so there's nothing new in that. She really gives me tremendous energy working with her because like me, inside, she's pretty wild about fooling around. You can saying anything to Diane. I've told other reporters because it just sticks in your mind, but sometimes, her preparation, I'll walk up to her and she'll look me in the eye and say, "You're disgusting." "What?" "You're disgusting." And it makes you laugh. She's a very original thinker, too, as a person.[2]

Diane Keaton had the same affection for Jack Nicholson, telling Murray in a separate interview,

> Well you know, working with Jack is sort of like standing in front of the Grand Canyon. I don't know, there's too much going on there and you're just this little speck on a precipice. He's like this huge, massive kind of structure. He's one of the Seven Wonders of the World. That's the way it feels. It feels like that because I think there's something about the way Jack uses language. It's like he's a master of the word, and the love of the word. A kiss is like you put the words away and you're just standing there and you're just sort of, "Oh, it's just you and me and we're really going to just experience this without saying anything." It's just beautiful. I loved it and I wish that I could do it again because it's like you just carry that with you. It was kind of a form of heaven.[3]

At this point, Jack Nicholson didn't need to choose projects to advance his career, so he simply tried to find roles and scripts that personally interested him. Usually, as an older man, he now explored parts that reflected his age. This romantic comedy does that. Nicholson plays a sixty-three-year-old man with an eye for women under thirty who falls for a woman who is fifty-six. The dynamic seems good when described, and Nicholson did like the script. He appreciated that writer-director Meyers had once worked for Billy Wilder. However, her other films, including *What Women Want* (2000) and, later, *It's Complicated* (2009), have the same sitcom-like structure and appear to offer the most stereotypical definition of the term *chick flick*. It depicts a life that is shallow, filled with heartbreak and mis-understanding, but cheekily ends with triumph after exacting some level of intellectual revenge.

The movie is commendable in that it is the rare romantic comedy that centers on an older couple. But the comedy mostly involves stupid jokes that just emphasize the fact that, hey, they're old. And then they don't even act like they are mature; the scenes after Harry stops living with Erica are just them going around and around in circles, refusing to say how they feel even though they're both obviously upset. Writing a play that is so directly based on their relationship just seems immature for a character who is supposed to be the opposite. However, it is worth mentioning that Keaton won a Golden Globe and was nominated for an Oscar for her performance. Nicholson does a good job with the material as well. He essentially plays a man who never really grew up, and is confronted by a lot of confused feelings when he does fall for Erica and realizes it may be time for him to finally take the next step.

At this point Jack Nicholson was losing interest in making movies. He still offered strong performances, even when the material was lackluster, as with this film and *Anger Management*. But despite responding to his own age and playing characters who were older, Nicholson was less enthusiastic about each project. At this point he had been in movies for fifty years (not counting his work in animation before he started working as a film actor). There was nothing more to prove. There didn't appear to be any further progression to his work, any more advancement for which he could reach. Jack Nicholson had managed to conquer every film genre as an actor, and enjoyed some success as a writer and even as a director.

However, and fortunately, his next film offered him another great character to play, one who had the sort of complexities he enjoyed investigating. And it allowed Nicholson to work with director Martin Scorsese for the first time. *The Departed* showed moviegoers that Jack Nicholson was still an actor who was not ready to rest lazily on his status as a screen icon.

THE DEPARTED

(2006, Warner Bros.)

★ ★ ★ ★

Director: Martin Scorsese
Screenplay: William Monahan
Producers: Brad Pitt, Brad Grey, Graham King. *Cinematographer:* Michael
    Ballhaus. *Editor:* Thelma Schoonmaker
Cast: Leonardo DiCaprio (Billy), Matt Damon (Colin Sullivan), Jack Nicholson
    (Frank Costello), Mark Wahlberg (Dignam), Martin Sheen (Queenan),
    Ray Winstone (French), Vera Farmiga (Madolyn), Anthony Anderson
    (Trooper Brown), Alec Baldwin (Ellergy), Kevin Corrigan (Cousin
    Sean), James Badge Dale (Trooper Barrigan), David O'Hara (Fitzy),
    Mark Rolston (Delahunt), Robert Wahlberg (Lazio), Kristen Dalton
    (Gwen), Thomas Duffy (Governor), J. C. MacKenzie (Realtor), Mary
    Klug (Billy's Aunt), Peg Holzemer (Mrs. Kennefick), Tracey Paleo
    (Darlene), Paula DeMers (Billy's Mother), Conor Donovan (Young
    Colin), Amanda Lynch (Carmen), Mick O'Rourke (Jimmy Bags),
    Deborah Carlson (Sister Mary Theresa), Paris Karonos (Jimmy
    Pappas), Francesca Scorsese (Little Girl at Airport)
Released: October 6, 2006
Specs: 151 minutes; color
Availability: DVD (Warner)

After two lackluster movies, Jack Nicholson came back with a brilliant performance in a great Martin Scorsese film. *The Departed* benefits from a creative directorial vision, a strong cast of top-drawer actors, and one of Jack Nicholson's finest performances. Director Martin Scorsese made a film that was inspired by the massively successful Hong Kong film *Internal Affairs* (2002).

Jack Nicholson is Frank Costello, an Irish-American gangster who runs a section in South Boston. Leonardo DiCaprio is Billy, an undercover cop who infiltrates organized crime. Matt Damon plays Sullivan, a mole for the mob who works for the police. Their lives intertwine in complex ways. Each becomes aware of the other, but although they know each other, neither realizes the other is the informant.

Billy gains Costello's confidence. Sullivan rises in the Special Investigation Unit. The complexities come from each man dealing with the stress of his double life. Each gathers information, makes plans, follows procedures, and reports information. They are working against each other in the same capacity from different perspectives. And, adding to the complexity of their connection, they are both involved with the same woman (a social worker for the police). When each is in danger of being caught, they must make sacrifices to save themselves.

With Leonardo DiCaprio in *The Departed*, the third Oscar-winning best picture Nicholson starred in. *Warner Bros. / Photofest © Warner Bros.*

The Departed is a film that can be discussed for its powerful screenplay, insightful direction, and any number of clever performances by so many members of its cast. However, our concentration for this book is on what Jack Nicholson offers. Nicholson often drew from past characters to inform the one he was currently doing, especially as he was continuing to establish himself. By the time of *The Departed*, coming in at the conclusion of his career, he was already able to define his work as he chose. However, for Frank Costello, Nicholson took a lot of what he got from the *Prizzi's Honor* experience and transformed it into this much different kind of gangster. Costello is so tough he wears a New York Yankees cap while wandering about Boston.

Nicholson stated in an interview for MTV,

> We wanted to take Marty's genre, the gangster thriller, and find a way to flat-out do it differently, and to push the envelope. And, well, we pushed it. Sometimes you don't say my main goal is to be original and breathtaking, because that puts too much pressure on you as an actor, but in this case, I felt that, in all honesty, that was what they hired me for.[1]

Nicholson's ability to play evil, unlikable characters and make them compelling and charismatic has been something of a stock-in-trade for the actor for some time. In a strong film filled with standout performances, Nicholson still manages to offer the best work. Peter Travers stated in *Rolling Stone*,

> Whether he's wielding a gun or a dildo, buying off cops, dissing Catholic priests as pederasts, seducing children into a life of crime, letting it snow cocaine on favored hookers or chatting while elbow-deep in blood, Nicholson is electrifying. Dispassionately executing a woman on a beach, Costello notes to his henchman Mr. French (a terrific Ray Winstone), "She fell funny." But Costello is no campy Joker. Channeling James Cagney in *White Heat* and Paul Muni in *Scarface*, Nicholson leeches out the glamour to create a landmark portrait of evil.[2]

Travers's comparison of Nicholson to Cagney is solid and accurate. In the film to which he refers, *White Heat* (1949), there is a scene where Cagney, as gangster Cody Jarrett, stands over a car, casually eating a chicken drumstick, and yells to the man he has stuffed in the trunk, asking how he is doing. The man says he needs air. Cody provides air by shooting holes into the trunk, thus killing the man inside. The way Cagney plays this elicits a laugh from the viewer, even though he is an unscrupulous killer who lapses into psychopathic episodes.

Frank Costello does not have psychopathic episodes. He, in fact, is a protected FBI informant, which is a revelation in the context of the film. When Sullivan confronts him about it, and then kills him, he is applauded by his fellow officers. Sullivan meets with Billy, whom he is recommending for a merit award, and asks the undercover cop if Frank ever said anything about an informant (still protecting his own identity). However, when Billy sees a recognizable envelope from Frank on Sullivan's desk, he realizes who the informant is. He offers CDs to the social worker, now living with Sullivan and pregnant with his child, and who realizes the truth about him.

While Damon and DiCaprio both play men who lead double lives, Nicholson has the difficult task of playing a character whose double life is not revealed to the audience. We must believe him to be the absolute crime lord, the one whose evil remains within the parameters of organized crime, with no connection to law enforcement of any kind. His identity is revealed by a secondary character within the course of the narrative. Nicholson, no stranger to complex characters, pulls this off handily. Leonardo DiCaprio recalled for Cole Smithey in an interview,

> Well, as far as Jack was concerned, we kind of expected the unexpected. We knew that Jack Nicholson joining up with Martin Scorsese to play a gangster is something that, I think, a lot of movie fans have been waiting for. For me, there were a number of different scenes where I had no idea what was going to happen. One scene in particular—we did the scene one way, and I remember Jack speaking to Marty because he didn't feel that he was intimidating enough. It was one of the table scenes. It was one of the most memorable moments of my life as far as being an actor is concerned. I remember coming into the scene one way, and then I came in the next day and the prop guy told me, "Be careful, he's got a fire extinguisher, a gun, some matches, and a bottle of whiskey." Ok, so some things are in the film that he did that day and some things aren't. I'm playing this guy that has to relay to the audience this constant 24 hour panic attack that I'm going through for my life, surrounded by people that would literally blow my head off if I gave them any indication of who I was, coupled with the fact that I'm sitting across the table from a homicidal maniac that will maybe light me on fire. It gives you, I don't want to say as an actor a sense of fear, but as a character a whole new dynamic. And it completely altered the scene in a completely different direction. I think we all knew that if he [Jack Nicholson] came on board that he would have to grab the reins with this character, and let him be freeform and we all were completely ready for that every day that we walked up on the set. He had a short run. He filmed his scenes and then he left, but those were some of the most intense moments of the film for me certainly, and as a human being as a person. There were some memories that I will never forget.[3]

Some of the strongest scenes in *The Departed* happen between Costello and Billy. The dialogue always presents the characters as a sort of master and apprentice.

Billy: You're seventy fucking years old. One of these guys is going to pop you. As for running drugs, what the fuck. You don't need the pain in the ass, and they're going to catch you. And you don't need the money.

Frank Costello: I haven't "needed the money" since I took Archie's milk money in the third grade. Tell you the truth, I don't need pussy any more either . . . but I like it.

Costello's expression of joy in his role as a leader in organized crime is borne out of dialogue like this, making the revelation that he is a protected federal informant that much more shocking. Costello also lets Billy know about the respect he always had for Billy's father.

Frank Costello: You know, if your father were alive, and saw you here sitting with me, let's say he would have a word with me about this. In fact, he'd kill seven guys just to cut my throat, and he could do it. That's maybe something you don't know about William Costigan Sr.

Billy: So he never? I mean, never?

Frank Costello: No. He kept his own counsel. He never wanted money. You can't do anything with a man like that.

Billy scoffs at Frank's suggestion that he perhaps consider returning to school. At this point neither knows the other's second identity.

Apparently Costello was based on noted gangster/FBI informant Whitey Bulger. Going into the film knowing that, one would think the revelation of Costello working for the FBI would be less of a shock, but it still is surprising because Nicholson does such a great job crafting this ruthless guy who you would think would want to stay as far away from police business as possible.

Nicholson plays Costello in the same manner as other volatile characters in his career, where he is uniformly low key but has the capacity to explode into a violent, hollering rage. The low-key quality is emphasized with the direction. For the opening scenes, Costello is only shown in shadows; we don't see his face. His own voiceover narrates his perspective, which introduces the character to the viewer:

I don't want to be a product of my environment. I want my environment to be a product of me. Years ago we had the church. That was only a way of saying—

we had each other. The Knights of Columbus were real head-breakers; true guineas. They took over their piece of the city. Twenty years after an Irishman couldn't get a fucking job, we had the presidency. May he rest in peace. That's what the niggers don't realize. If I got one thing against the black chappies, it's this—no one gives it to you. You have to take it.

It is a method that Scorsese had used before, most notably in *Goodfellas* (1990) and *Casino* (1994), two films that thrive on their narration. Frank Costello is immediately gritty, uncompromising, bitter, and violent. He strikes an intimidating figure.

Apparently Nicholson was given a lot of freedom to improvise, and a lot of that earlier exchange with Billy was ad-libbed. It's interesting to see the touches Nicholson put on Costello that really make the character so much more menacing. For instance, at one point during that conversation with Billy he pulls out the gun and starts swinging it around—that was not in the script. It's also interesting to see the relationships develop between him and Billy and between him and Sullivan—Costello is like a father figure to them both.

By the time of *The Departed* it had become Hollywood lore that Martin Scorsese never won an Oscar, despite being nominated for such brilliant works as *Raging Bull* (1980) or the aforementioned films that quickly became classics. *The Departed* changed that, and Mr. Scorsese won an Oscar. The film also won for Best Picture, Best Screenplay, and Best Editing, and received a Best Supporting Actor nomination for Mark Wahlberg's outstanding performance as Dignam, who neatly wraps up the film after having functioned as its voice of judgment throughout.

Critics praised the film and its performances, especially Nicholson's work. Roger Ebert stated,

> It's strange that Jack Nicholson and Scorsese have never worked together, since they seem like a natural fit; he makes Frank Costello not a godfather, not a rat, not a blowhard, but a smart man who finally encounters a situation no one could fight free of, because he simply lacks all the necessary information.[4]

Richard Corliss stated for *Time* magazine,

> Frank, played by Nicholson, is a juicy creation, a mobster who revels in his connoisseurship of executive violence. ("One of us had to die," he says of a gangland face-off. "With me it's usually the other one.") He has words of wisdom for a thug who says his mother is near death. "So we all are," Frank observes. "Act accordingly." In Billy he sees a bright, focused young man with

ambitions, though Frank misreads them. "You wanna be me," he tells the kid, who replies, honestly for once, "I probably 'could' be you. But I don't 'wanna' be you."[5]

The Departed had a $90 million budget, half of which was used to pay the actors. The film was a massive success and grossed nearly $300 million at the box office. Since Jack Nicholson was seriously considering ending his film career around this time, *The Departed* might have been a perfect culmination. Instead he accepted the opportunity to play in a comedy because he was attracted to many elements regarding its production. It also continued Nicholson's decision to play older characters who were around his own age. Rob Reiner's *The Bucket List* would be about dying men fulfilling a few dreams before they go. Before filming began on *The Bucket List*, Nicholson told Josh Horowitz for MTV,

> I thought it was very adventurous of Rob to think about making a comedy about dying. And I like to be adventurous. It has got to be a very personal film. It's got a lot of things in it that people think about that aren't articulated. For that reason, it's got some good spunk to it. And of course, if you're going to make a comedy, you better make them laugh. I don't want to jinx myself, but I feel pretty good about it.[6]

THE BUCKET LIST

(2008, Warner Bros.)

★ ★

Director: Rob Reiner
Screenplay: Justin Zackham
Producers: Rob Reiner, Craig Zadan, Alan Griesman, Neil Meron.
   Cinematographer: John Schwartzman. *Editor:* Robert Leighton
Cast: Jack Nicholson (Edward), Morgan Freeman (Carter), Sean Hayes
   (Thomas), Beverly Todd (Virginia), Rob Morrow (Dr. Hollins),
   Alfonso Freeman (Roger), Roweena King (Angelica), Annton Berry Jr.
   (Kai), Verda Bridgers (Chandra), Destiny Brownridge (Maya), Brian
   Copeland (Lee), Ian Anthony Dale (Instructor), Jennifer DeFrancisco
   (Emily), Jonathan Hernandez (Manny), Andrea J. Johnson (Elizabeth)
Released: December 16, 2007
Specs: 97 minutes; color
Availability: DVD (Warner)

What could have been a movie of inspiration and triumph, *The Bucket List* turns out to be depressing and sophomoric. Morgan Freeman and Jack Nicholson star as Carter and Edward, two men suffering from terminal cancer who find themselves bonding when they are in the same hospital room. Edward is wealthy; Carter is hard working but comfortable from his savings. They decide to make a "bucket list"—things they'd like to do before they "kick the bucket." Most of the rest of the movie is them engaging in these various activities. There are tangible things like "go skydiving" to intangible ones like the vague "kiss the most beautiful girl in the world." Some are played for comic effect, while others attempt to be insightful but come off as mawkish.

It is unfortunate. The actors are outstanding and the general idea is good, with the potential for an honest, positive message about living life to the fullest and not waiting until you are near death before you turn your dreams into goals and, eventually, accomplishments. However, as Stephen Holden's review in the *New York Times* stated,

> Saddest of all, the professed spiritual goals on the pair's checklist of things to do—"laugh till you cry," "witness something majestic"—are the kind of pallid bromides found in the pages of a quickie self-help book: "I'm Not O.K., and Neither Are You."[1]

The development of the characters is good. Carter has been a working-class garage mechanic for half a century, but he has a knowledge of history that is so vast, his coworkers delight in quizzing him, attempting to stump him. They never succeed. Carter wanted to be a history teacher, but it never happened because he was "black, broke, and had a baby on the way." He was content with having worked hard and provided for his family. Edward is a rather loudmouthed corporate billionaire who says things like, "My first wife thought mayonnaise came from a plant," and refers to his

Morgan Freeman and Nicholson face mortality together in *The Bucket List*. Warner Bros. / Photofest © Warner Bros.

second wife as "the sequel." He also makes reference to a daughter, with whom he has no contact.

Any consistent fun one can get out of their exploits is usually sidetracked by events like sudden dramatics, complications of their illness (during dinner at a fancy restaurant, Carter must leave abruptly because a heart catheter comes loose and his shirt is stained with blood). There is also a tangential conflict with Carter's wife, who is chagrined that her husband has run off with this veritable stranger with the little time he has left. The film is uneven, wavering between the comic and the serious, and rather than blending cohesively, these elements tend to clash. Much of Carter's and Edward's behavior is unrealistic; it is hard to believe that someone like Carter would decide out of the blue to travel the world with a stranger instead of his family. The fact that Edward is rich and can afford whatever venture they decide to undertake seems a bit too convenient.

Along with being uneven in its narrative structure, *The Bucket List* is also filled with scenes that drag to the point of dullness. The characters sit around and talk a lot, coming to grips with their lives, their existence, their purpose, their legacy, and other such end-of-life issues. They travel throughout the world, enjoying exploits in Paris, Hong Kong, and other remote places, but it could just be a series of upscale restaurants in New York or Chicago.

When Edward is told by Carter that he never made love to anyone other than his wife, Edward arranges for Carter to be approached by a beautiful woman. Carter demurs. When Carter arranges for their driver to take them to the home of Edward's daughter, an angry Edward does not appreciate the surprise and storms off. These are presented as highlights, but they are not funny or impactful. They're just scenes that lie there in the context of the story.

Roger Ebert, then suffering from the cancer that would end his life five years later, stated in his review,

> *The Bucket List* thinks dying of cancer is a laff riot followed by a dime-store epiphany. The sole redeeming merit of the film is the steady work by Morgan Freeman, who has appeared in more than one embarrassing movie, but never embarrassed himself. Maybe it's not Jack Nicholson's fault that his role cries out to be overplayed, but it's his fate, and ours.[2]

Nicholson does not appear to overact any more than what the character seems to call for, and his character is not really much different than the one he played in *Something's Gotta Give*. However, even potentially strong scenes, like his farewell to Carter, whose cancer has spread to his brain, or when he reconnects with his daughter and meets his new granddaughter, whom he kisses, and then crosses "kiss the most beautiful girl" off the list, are emotionally insufficient. Carter and Edward accomplishing "laugh till you cry" while Carter lies dying in a hospital bed is another moment that falls far short of its potential. That ending feels like it drags on too long, just to milk as much sentiment out of the story as possible. There is a nice sequence with Carter's voiceover reading his final letter to Edward, followed by the scene where Edward meets his granddaughter, but they follow it up with a wailing, emotional speech from Edward at Carter's funeral that was just too much. The movie would have ended more effectively before that happened.

Nicholson told Steve Weintraub in an interview that he felt director Rob Reiner managed to make this difficult subject both funny and moving, stating,

> Well, you know, I'd worked with Rob and I liked working with him and Morgan and I have known one another at a distance for a long time and had always known we wanted to work together, and that's pretty much all it took for me. That was that and off we went. Plus, it's a tough little puzzle. Rob found the tone for this fairly early on. He said we're not going to make this movie nine times; let's try and get it right. To deal with this subject, one of the most fearsome subjects in a comic manner is a creative puzzle really. Until I saw it with the first audience, you can't really know if you veered on or off. My impression from the first screening was that I was impressed with how long the audience was moved at the end of the picture. It wasn't just they were moved. When you've got an audience going for 10–15 minutes that's a long time. And I don't think you can do that if you're sentimental, particularly these are semi-professional audiences. It has sentiment, but if you get sentimental you're going to lose them. So hats off. We kind of throw it at the wall and Rob got it good. He did a good job really.[3]

The Bucket List had a pretty large budget of $45 million but was a box-office hit, earning over $175 million. This amounts to a success in the eyes of Hollywood filmmakers. But it was a real waste of talent for its actors and its directors. The only reason it is essential to the Jack Nicholson filmography is because it was a big hit, as well as what he believed to be his penultimate film.

HOW DO YOU KNOW

(2010, Columbia Pictures)

★ ★

Director: James L. Brooks
Screenplay: James L. Brooks
Producers: James L. Brooks, Julie Ansell, Paula Weinstein. *Cinematographer:*
    Janusz Kamiński. *Editor:* Richard Marks
Cast: Reese Witherspoon (Lisa), Paul Rudd (George), Owen Wilson (Matty),
    Jack Nicholson (Charles), Kathryn Hahn (Annie), Mark Linn-Baker
    (Ron), Lenny Venito (Al), Molly Price (Coach Sally), Ron McLarty
    (George's Lawyer), Shelley Conn (Terry), Teyonah Paris (Riva), Tony
    Shaloub (Psychiatrist), Dean Norris (Softball Coach), Jim Bouton
    (cameo)
Released: December 17, 2010
Specs: 116 minutes; color
Availability: DVD (Columbia)

After being off screen for three years, Jack Nicholson agreed to appear in his friend James L. Brooks's next movie project. *How Do You Know* is a rather tepid romantic comedy that benefits from a good cast but is missing the witty dialogue necessary to make any movie of this genre effective. It is a lightweight vehicle that is only essential to Jack Nicholson's filmography because it is his last film. Upon completion, Nicholson stopped making movies and indicated he has little interest in ever doing so again.

How Do You Know features Reese Witherspoon as Lisa, a softball player who finds she will not be on the Team US roster. While contemplating just where to go with her life from here, Lisa hooks up with major league pitcher Matty (Owen Wilson) and young executive George (Paul Rudd). The usual conflict ensues, as both vie for Lisa's attention. George has just been fired from a company run by his father after being accused of malfeasance during a federal investigation. His initial date with Lisa is a failure because of his constant whining over his job situation. Meanwhile, Matty is wealthy, successful, but unreliable. Lisa is not the only woman he is seeing.

Nicholson's contribution to this movie is in the role of George's father. Sadly, his character is pretty much pointless. According to Roger Ebert in his *Chicago Sun-Times* review,

> I expected this movie to be better. The writer-director is James L. Brooks, and this is the fourth time he's worked with Jack Nicholson (after *Terms of Endearment* and *As Good as It Gets*, which both brought him acting Oscars). So let's start with Nicholson. Brooks hasn't given him much to work with. Here he plays a conniving tycoon who doesn't deserve his son's loyalty. It's a heavy role, and there's little to lighten it. In his best roles, Jack always seems to be getting away with something. He is here, too, but it's not funny. We like to identify with his onscreen sins, and this is a rare time when Nicholson is simply a creep.[1]

Although he once again settles comfortably into the role of an older character, and his wily charm does successfully manipulate his son in the film, who may face prison time after being indicted, Jack Nicholson is far less effective here than usual. Because this character is so utterly familiar to him, he offers little effort beyond what was on paper.

However, according to James L. Brooks, that was the intention. An icon like Jack Nicholson casts a long shadow, so he must be more reserved in a role such as this so as not to take the spotlight from the leading players—Witherspoon, Owen Wilson as the pitcher, and Paul Rudd as Jack's son. Brooks told *Esquire*,

> I had an argument years and years ago with another comedy writer. Jack Nicholson and Dustin Hoffman were the biggest guns at the time—long may they wave—and we had an argument about which one was number one. I took Jack, and I finally won the argument by saying he could play either role in *The Odd Couple*.[2]

Nicholson with Paul Rudd in his third film for director James L. Brooks. *Columbia Pictures / Photofest © Columbia Pictures*

In interviews, Nicholson supported the fact that he had a smaller supporting role, telling Louise Gannon for the *Daily Mail*,

I am from a different era of movie acting. My career doesn't depend on explosions and pyrotechnics. What I liked about this script is that the same rules apply. It hasn't got people flying off walls and lots of guns and yelling. It's a movie that's based on a good script and good acting, and it's supposed to move you. It's the sort of movie I want to be a part of. In these times people need to be able to laugh.[3]

Coming from James L. Brooks and knowing his past successes with Nicholson, it is especially disappointing that this movie is such a misfire. The story had potential; all of the characters are appropriately screwed up, and it doesn't exactly follow the typical romantic comedy formula. But there's little comedy, and little romance, as the cast just doesn't have enough spark between them to conjure up believable relationships. It's not really their fault, though, as they weren't given good material to work with in the first place.

How Do You Know had quite a hefty budget. Reese Witherspoon was paid $15 million, Jack Nicholson received $12 million, Owen Wilson got $10 million, and Paul Rudd earned $3 million. Combined with Brooks's fee, that totaled about $50 million just in those salaries. Brooks also had a slow, methodical way of working, which contributed to the increased budget. The film ended up costing $100 million to make, and its worldwide gross was less than half that amount.

Judging by the weakness of this film and the previous *The Bucket List*, it is unfortunate that if Nicholson's intention was indeed to retire from making movies, he didn't choose to conclude with *The Departed*. Instead, *How Do You Know* is his final film at the time of this writing.

AFTERWORD

Jack Nicholson made no formal announcement that he retired from films after the 2010 release of *How Do You Know*. Jason Chester of the *Daily Mail* stated,

> Jack was rumored to have unofficially retired from the acting business last year after suffering from memory loss. A source told RadarOnline: "Quite frankly, at 76, Jack has memory issues and can no longer remember the lines being asked of him. His memory isn't what it used to be." Jack was said to have turned down the role of an aging alcoholic father in 2013 hit *Nebraska*, with the lead eventually going to Bruce Dern—whose performance has earned him an Academy Award nomination for Best Actor in a Leading Role. But while Jack appears to be keeping a low profile, the Hollywood insider claims he isn't leaving his beloved profession behind entirely. "Jack has no intention of retiring from the limelight," says the source. "He's not retiring from public life, at all. He just doesn't want a tribute. He's happy to tacitly join the retirees club like Sean Connery."[1]

Nicholson has spent years between movie projects in the past, and it could very well be that he will choose to appear in another movie even after the release of this book. As indicated in this book's Introduction, Robert Downey Jr. has twice attempted to lure Jack Nicholson back in front of the camera, but to no avail. It is interesting to speculate how much different

Nebraska or *The Judge* might have been if Nicholson had taken the roles that later went to Bruce Dern and Robert Duvall.

Nicholson also contemplated his mortality, especially as more and more friends passed away. He told the *Daily Mail*,

> One of the toughest parts of ageing is losing your friends. At first it starts quietly, then pretty soon it's every month, and you can't help but think, "When is that bell going to go off for me?" And on top of that you feel this constant loss. At this time of life, you feel just a sword's point from death. It's frightening—who wants to face God and the clear white light? I know I definitely don't. Yet.[2]

Jack Nicholson is very likely the finest actor in the American cinema's modern era. As we looked over his essential films, from his debut in fascinating B films for the likes of Roger Corman and Monte Hellman, to his emergence as a star, to his eventual status as an icon, our understanding of the depth of his talent, the extension of his ability, is that it is far more impressive than that of many perfectly capable actors in American film.

It could be said that luck had something to do with it, Nicholson having been granted the opportunity to star in so many movies that have become classics. But it could just as easily be said that those movies are classics in large part due to Nicholson's performances and his ability to breathe life into the most complex of characters.

Jack Nicholson redefined stardom, redefined the concept of the leading man, redefined the award winner, and redefined what an icon represented. Brash, quirky, insightful, charismatic, and immensely talented, the films of Jack Nicholson will continue to enlighten, inspire, and entertain for as long as future generations continue to explore the motion picture's rich history.

NOTES

INTRODUCTION

1. Singer, Matt. "To Clarify, Jack Nicholson Is Not Retired, He's Just Not Interested in Making More Movies." *The Dissolve*, September 16, 2013.
2. Hicks, Tony. "Robert Downey Jr. Wants Jack Nicholson out of Retirement." *San Jose Mercury News*, May 1, 2014.

PROLOGUE

1. Collins, Nancy. "The Great Seducer: Jack Nicholson." *Rolling Stone*, March 29, 1984.
2. Manasquan High School now has a theater and a drama award named for him.
3. From *The Teacher: The Memoir of Blacklisted Actor and Teacher to the Stars, Jeff Corey*. Michelle Cohen Projects, http://www.michellecohenprojects.com/the-teacher-the-memoir-of-blacklisted-actor-and-teacher-to-the-stars-jeff-corey/.
4. Walker, Beverly. "The Bird Is on His Own." *Film Comment*, May–June 1985.
5. Walker, "The Bird Is on His Own."

CHAPTER 1

1. Barnes, Daniel. "The Cry Baby Killer." *Sacramento News and Review*, January 4, 2007.

CHAPTER 2

1. Corman, Roger. *How I Made a Hundred Movies in Hollywood and Never Lost a Dime*. Boston: Da Capo Press, 1998, pp. 61–62, 67–70.

2. Corman, *How I Made a Hundred Movies in Hollywood*, pp. 61–62, 67–70.

3. *Variety* staff, "The Little Shop of Horrors," *Variety*, September 30, 1960.

CHAPTER 3

1. *Variety* staff. "The Raven." *Variety*, January 31, 1963.

2. Staff writer. "The Raven." *Independent Exhibitor's Film Bulletin*, February 4, 1963.

CHAPTER 4

1. French, Lawrence. *The Making of "The Raven": "The Raven" Novelisation by Eunice Sudak, Based on Script by Richard Matheson*. Bear Manor Media, 2012.

2. Robey, Tim. "Roger Corman Interview." *Telegraph*, November 6, 2013.

3. Smith, Richard Harlan. "The Terror." Turner Classic Movies, www.tcm.com.

4. McGee, Mark. *Faster and Furiouser: The Revised and Fattened Fable of American International Pictures*. Jefferson, NC: McFarland, 1996.

CHAPTER 5

1. Sorrento, Matthew. "A Rebel Rides Again: An Interview with Monte Hellman on *The Shooting* (1966) and *Ride in the Whirlwind* (1966)." *Film International* 12, no. 4 (2014).

2. Eliot, Marc. *Nicholson: A Biography*. New York: Crown Archetype, 2013, p. 46.

3. Walker, Beverly. "Interview: Jack Nicholson." *Film Comment*, May–June 1985.

CHAPTER 6

1. Sorrento, Matthew. "A Rebel Rides Again: An Interview with Monte Hellman on *The Shooting* (1966) and *Ride in the Whirlwind* (1966)." *Film International* 12, no. 4 (2014).

2. Sorrento, Matthew. "A Rebel Rides Again."

3. McGilligan, Patrick. *Jack's Life: A Biography of Jack Nicholson*. New York: W. W. Norton, 1994.

4. Sobczynski, Peter. "Existential Westerns: Criterion Editions of 'The Shooting,' 'Ride in the Whirlwind.'" RogerEbert.com, November 26, 2014.

CHAPTER 7

1. *Variety* staff. "Head." *Variety*, November 6, 1968.

2. Canby, Vincent. "Head." *New York Times*, November 7, 1968.

3. "Exclusive: Michael Nesmith Remembers Davy Jones." *Rolling Stone*, March 8, 2012.

CHAPTER 9

1. Greenspun, Roger. "Five Easy Pieces." *New York Times*, September 12, 1970.

2. Ebert, Roger. "Five Easy Pieces." Great Movies page at RogertEbert.com, March 16, 2003.

CHAPTER 10

1. Ebert, Roger. "Drive, He Said." *Chicago Sun-Times*, January 1, 1972.

2. Canby, Vincent. "Drive, He Said." *New York Times*, June 14, 1971.

3. Ann-Margret. *Ann-Margret—My Story*. New York: Putnam, 1994, p. 208.

4. Ebert, Roger. "Carnal Knowledge." *Chicago Sun-Times*, July 6, 1971.

5. Ann-Margret, *Ann-Margret*, p. 210.

CHAPTER 11

1. In fact, director Hal Ashby purposely shot in sequence to make it easier for newcomer Quaid to play his role.

2. According to the Internet Movie Database, the word "fuck" was used sixty-five times, which was, at this time, a record. An alternate version, where the language was toned down, was shot simultaneously for television broadcast.

3. Starr, T. "High on the Future." *Ticketron Entertainment*, June–July 1973.

4. Canby, Vincent. "'Last Detail' a Comedy of Sailors on Shore." *New York Times*, February 11, 1974.

5. *The Last Detail* financial information is from The Numbers website, http://www.the-numbers.com/movie/Last-Detail-The#tab=news.

CHAPTER 12

1. Horowitz, Josh. "Jack Nicholson Talks! In Rare Interview, Actor Reveals Details of Never-Shot 'Chinatown' Sequel." MTV.com, November 5, 2007.

2. Horowitz, "Jack Nicholson Talks!"

3. Canby, Vincent. "Chinatown." *New York Times*, June 21, 1974.

4. Ebert, Roger. "Chinatown." *Chicago Sun-Times*, June 21, 1974.

5. Berardinelli, James. "Chinatown (United States, 1974)." ReelViews movie reviews website, http://www.reelviews.net/reelviews/chinatown.

6. Reeves, Carson. "Chinatown: Best Screenplay Ever?" *ScriptShadow* (blog), February 17, 2011. http://scriptshadow.blogspot.com/2011/02/chinatown-best-screenplay-ever.html

CHAPTER 13

1. Hametz, Aljean. "The Nurse Who Rules the Cuckoo's Nest." *New York Times*, November 30, 1975.

2. Canby, Vincent. "One Flew over the Cuckoo's Nest." *New York Times*, November 28, 1975.

3. Rafferty, Terrence. "A Storied Life." *DGA Quarterly*, Fall 2008.

CHAPTER 14

1. McGilligan, Patrick. *Jack's Life: A Biography of Jack Nicholson*. New York: W. W. Norton, 1994.

2. McGilligan, *Jack's Life*.

3. *Variety* staff. "Goin' South." *Variety*, October 6, 1978.

CHAPTER 15

1. Cut to 119 minutes for European release.

2. Danko, Meredith. "25 Things You Might Not Know about 'The Shining.'" *Mental Floss*, April 1, 2014.

3. Originally, Kubrick had used a fake door for Nicholson to bust through with the ax. But Nicholson had once been a volunteer firefighter and broke through the door too quickly and easily. A real door had to be used.

4. Norden, Eric. "The Stephen King Playboy Interview." *Playboy*, June 1983.

5. Ebert, Roger. "Interview with Shelley Duvall." *Chicago Sun-Times*, December 14, 1980.

6. Daniel, Hugo, and Daniel Beekman. "All Work and No Play." *New York Daily News*, October 7, 2013.

7. Maslin, Janet. "The Shining." *New York Times*, May 23, 1980.

CHAPTER 16

1. Biskind, Peter. "Thunder on the Left." *Vanity Fair*, March 2006.

2. Biskind, "Thunder on the Left."

CHAPTER 17

1. Ebert, Roger. "Interview with Jack Nicholson." *Chicago Sun-Times*, November 27, 1983.

2. Ebert, "Interview with Jack Nicholson."

3. "Burt Reynolds Discusses His Career in Showbiz." *Larry King Live*, February 23, 2000.

4. Schruers, Fred. "Jack Nicholson: The Rolling Stone Interview." *Rolling Stone*. August 14, 1986.

5. Ebert, "Interview with Jack Nicholson."

6. Maslin, Janet. "Terms of Endearment." *New York Times*, November 23, 1983.

7. Associated Press. "Shirley MacLaine, 80, Reflects on Her Legacy." *Daily Mail*, November 1, 2014.

CHAPTER 18

1. Kael, Pauline. "Prizzi's Honor." *New Yorker*, June 1985.

2. Benson, Sheila. "Prizzi's Honor." *Los Angeles Times*, June 14, 1985.

3. *Variety* staff. "Prizzi's Honor." *Variety*, June 16, 1985.

4. Walker, Beverly. "Interview: Jack Nicholson." *Film Comment*, May–June 1985.

5. Walker, "Interview."

CHAPTER 19

1. Geringer, Dan. "Life's Just Been a Witch for 'Eastwick' Star Cher." *Philadelphia Daily News*, June 11, 1987.

2. Maslin, Janet. "The Witches of Eastwick." *New York Times*, June 12, 1987.

3. Bogdanovich, Peter. Interview. *Suddeutsche Zeitung Magazin*, November 2006.

CHAPTER 20

1. Ryan, Michael. "The Making of 'Ironweed.'" *People*, January 18, 1988.
2. Ebert, Roger. "Ironweed." *Chicago Sun-Times*, February 12, 1988.
3. Maslin, Janet. "Ironweed." *New York Times*, December 18, 1987.
4. Benson, Sheila. "Ironweed." *Los Angeles Times*, December 18, 1987.

CHAPTER 21

1. Horowitz, Josh. "Jack Nicholson 'Furious.'" *MTV News*, November 6, 2007.
2. Boucher, Geoff. "Michael Keaton's Dark Memories of 'Batman.'" *Los Angeles Times*, May 12, 2011.
3. Canby, Vincent. "Batman." *New York Times*, June 23, 1989.
4. Howe, Desson. "The Two Jakes." *Washington Post*, August 10, 1990.

CHAPTER 22

1. Bailey, David. "Bailey's Heroes." *GQ*, March 2014.
2. Canby, Vincent. "A Few Good Men." *New York Times*, December 11, 1992.
3. Ebert, Roger. "A Few Good Men." *Chicago Sun-Times*, December 11, 1992.

CHAPTER 23

1. Andrew, Geoff. "Wolf." *Time Out Film Guide*. London: Time Out Publishers. 2010.

CHAPTER 24

1. Ebert Roger. "Jack Nicholson: On a Collision Course with Fate." *Chicago Sun-Times*, November 26, 1995.
2. Belk, Melissa, and Graham Fuller. "New Again: Sean Penn." *Interview*, November 7, 2012.
3. Maslin, Janet. "The Crossing Guard." *New York Times,* November 15, 1995.

4. Turan, Kenneth. "The Crossing Guard." *Los Angeles Times*, November 15, 1995.

CHAPTER 25

1. Howe, Desson. "As Good as It Gets." *Washington Post*, December 23, 1997.

CHAPTER 26

1. "Pledge, The: Interview with Jack Nicholson." Cinema.com.
2. "Pledge, The."
3. Holden, Stephen. "The Pledge." *New York Times*, January 19, 2001.

CHAPTER 27

1. Rainer, Peter. "About Schmidt." *New York*, December 16, 2002.
2. Kennedy, Dana. "I Have a Sweet Spot for What's Attractive to Me." *Guardian*, October 3, 2002.

CHAPTER 28

1. Lee, Alana. "Adam Sandler Interview." *BBC*, October 28, 2014.
2. Ebert, Roger. "Anger Management." *Chicago Sun-Times,* April 11, 2003.
3. Mitchell, Elvis. "Anger Management." *New York Times,* April 11, 2003.

CHAPTER 29

1. Orr, Christopher. "Something's Gotta Give." *Atlantic*, May 4, 2004.
2. Murray, Rebecca. "Jack Nicholson Interview." About.com.
3. Murray, Rebecca. "Diane Keaton Interview." About.com.

CHAPTER 30

1. Horowitz, Josh. "Jack Nicholson Talks!" MTV.com, November 5, 2007.
2. Travers, Peter. "The Departed." *Rolling Stone*, September 28, 2006.

3. Smithey, Cole. "Leonardo DiCaprio Interview." ColeSmithey.com, October 11, 2006.

4. Ebert, Roger. "The Departed." Great Movies page at RogerEbert.com, July 5, 2007.

5. Corliss, Richard. "The Departed." *Time*, October 1, 2006.

6. Horowitz, "Jack Nicholson Talks!"

CHAPTER 31

1. Holden, Stephen. "The Bucket List." *New York Times*, December 25, 2007.

2. Ebert, Roger. "The Bucket List." *Chicago Sun-Times*, January 8, 2008.

3. Weintraub, Steve. "Jack Nicholson and Morgan Freeman Interview." *Collider*, December 23, 2007.

CHAPTER 32

1. Ebert, Roger. "Prizzi's Honor." *Chicago Sun-Times*, December 17, 2010.

2. Fussman, Cal. "James L. Brooks: What I've Learned." *Esquire*, December 17, 2010.

3. Gannon, Louise. "The Melancholy Confessions of Jack Nicholson." *Daily Mail*, January 31, 2011.

AFTERWORD

1. Chaster, Jason. "Out and a Pout!" *Daily Mail*, January 29, 2014.

2. Gannon, Louise. "The Melancholy Confessions of Jack Nicholson." *Daily Mail*, January 31, 2011.

BIBLIOGRAPHY

BOOKS

Brode, Douglas. *The Films of Jack Nicholson*. Metuchen, NJ: Citadel, 1986.

Corman, Roger. *How I Made a Hundred Movies in Hollywood and Never Lost a Dime*. Boston: Da Capo Press, 1998.

Douglas, Edward. *Jack: The Great Seducer*. New York: HarperCollins, 2004.

Eliot, Marc. *Nicholson: A Biography*. New York: Crown Archetype, 2013.

Forman, Milos. *Turnaround: A Memoir*. New York: Villard, 1994.

French, Lawrence. *The Making of "The Raven": The Raven Novelisation by Eunice Sudak, Based on Script by Richard Matheson*. Bear Manor Media, 2012.

Margret, Ann. *Ann-Margret—My Story*. New York: Putnam, 1994.

McGee, Mark. *Faster and Furiouser: The Revised and Fattened Fable of American International Pictures*. Jefferson, NC: McFarland, 1996.

McGilligan, Patrick. *Jack's Life: A Biography of Jack Nicholson*. New York: W. W. Norton, 1994.

Ray, Fred Olen. *The New Poverty Row: Independent Filmmakers as Distributors*. Jefferson, NC: McFarland, 1991.

Thompson, Peter. *Jack Nicholson: The Life and Times of an Actor on the Edge*. Secaucus, NJ: Birch Lane Press, 1997.

Wiley, Mason, and Damien Bona. *Inside Oscar*. New York: Ballantine, 1996.

ARTICLES

Associated Press. "Shirley MacLaine, 80, Reflects on Her Legacy." *Daily Mail*, November 1, 2014.

Bailey, David. "Bailey's Heroes." *GQ*, March 2014.

Belk, Melissa, and Graham Fuller. "New Again: Sean Penn." *Interview*, November 7, 2012.

Biskind, Peter. "Thunder on the Left." *Vanity Fair*, March 2006.

Bogdanovich, Peter. Interview. *Suddeutsche Zeitung Magazin.* November 2006.

Boucher, Geoff. "Michael Keaton's Dark Memories of 'Batman.'" *Los Angeles Times*, May 12, 2011.

Chaster, Jason. "Out and a Pout!" *Daily Mail*, January 29, 2014.

Collins, Nancy. "The Great Seducer: Jack Nicholson." *Rolling Stone*, March 29, 1984.

Daniel, Hugo, and Daniel Beekman. "All Work and No Play." *New York Daily News*, October 7, 2013.

Danko, Meredith. "25 Things You Might Not Know about 'The Shining.'" *Mental Floss*, April 1, 2014.

Ebert, Roger. "Interview with Jack Nicholson." *Chicago Sun-Times*, November 27, 1983.

Ebert, Roger. "Interview with Shelley Duvall." *Chicago Sun-Times*, December 14, 1980.

Ebert Roger. "Jack Nicholson: On a Collision Course with Fate." *Chicago Sun-Times*, November 26, 1995.

Gannon, Louise. "The Melancholy Confessions of Jack Nicholson." *Daily Mail*, January 31, 2011.

Geringer, Dan. "Life's Just Been a Witch for 'Eastwick' Star Cher." *Philadelphia Daily News*, June 11, 1987.

Hicks, Tony. "Robert Downey Jr. Wants Jack Nicholson out of Retirement." *San Jose Mercury News*, May 1, 2014.

Kennedy, Dana. "I Have a Sweet Spot for What's Attractive to Me." *Guardian*, October 3, 2002.

Lee, Alana. "Adam Sandler Interview." *BBC*, October 28, 2014.

Murphy, Sean. "'Five Easy Pieces' Must Be Appreciated on Its Own Cantakerous Terms." *Pop Matters*, July 30, 2015.

Norden, Eric. "The Stephen King Playboy Interview." *Playboy*, June 1983.

Rafferty, Terrence. "A Storied Life." *DGA Quarterly*, Fall 2008.

Robey, Tim. "Roger Corman Interview." *The Telegraph*, November 6, 2013.

Rolling Stone. "Exclusive: Michael Nesmith Remembers Davy Jones." March 8, 2012.

Ryan, Michael. "The Making of 'Ironweed.'" *People*, January 18, 1988.

Schruers, Fred. "Jack Nicholson: The Rolling Stone Interview." *Rolling Stone*, August 14, 1986.

Singer, Matt. "To Clarify, Jack Nicholson Is Not Retired, He's Just Not Interested in Making More Movies." *The Dissolve*, September 16, 2013.

Sorrento, Matthew. "A Rebel Rides Again: An Interview with Monte Hellman on *The Shooting* (1966) and *Ride in the Whirlwind* (1966)." *Film International* 12, no. 4 (2014).

Starr, T. "High on the Future." *Ticketron Entertainment*, June–July 1973.

Walker, Beverly. "The Bird Is on His Own." *Film Comment*, May–June 1985.

Walker, Beverly. "Interview: Jack Nicholson." *Film Comment*, May–June 1985.

Weintraub, Steve. "Jack Nicholson and Morgan Freeman Interview." *Collider*, December 23, 2007.

Weldon, Michael. "Jack Hill Interview." *Psychotronic*, Summer 1992.

REVIEWS

Andrew, Geoff. "Wolf." *Time Out Film Guide*. London: Time Out Publishers, 2010.

Barnes, Daniel. "The Cry Baby Killer." *Sacramento News and Review*, January 4, 2007.

Benson, Sheila. "Ironweed." *Los Angeles Times*, December 18, 1987.

Benson, Sheila. "Prizzi's Honor." *Los Angeles Times*, June 14, 1985.

Canby, Vincent. "Chinatown." *New York Times*, June 21, 1974.

Canby, Vincent. "Drive, He Said." *New York Times*, June 14, 1971.

Canby, Vincent. "A Few Good Men." *New York Times*, December 11, 1992.

Canby, Vincent. "Head." *New York Times*, November 7, 1968

Canby, Vincent. "One Flew over the Cuckoo's Nest." *New York Times*, November 28, 1975.

Corliss, Richard. "The Departed." *Time*, October 1, 2006.

Ebert, Roger. "Anger Management." *Chicago Sun-Times*, April 11, 2003.

Ebert, Roger. "The Bucket List." *Chicago Sun-Times*, January 8, 2008.

Ebert, Roger. "Carnal Knowledge." *Chicago Sun-Times*, July 6, 1971.

Ebert, Roger. "Chinatown." *Chicago Sun-Times*, June 21, 1974.

Ebert, Roger. "Drive, He Said." *Chicago Sun-Times*, January 1, 1972.

Ebert, Roger. "A Few Good Men." *Chicago Sun-Times*, December 11, 1992.

Ebert, Roger. "Ironweed." *Chicago Sun-Times*, February 12, 1988.

Greenspun, Roger. "Five Easy Pieces." *New York Times*, September 12, 1970.

Holden, Stephen. "The Bucket List." *New York Times*, December 25, 2007.

Holden, Stephen. "The Pledge." *New York Times*, January 19, 2001.

Howe, Desson. "As Good as It Gets." *Washington Post*, December 23, 1997.

Howe, Desson. "The Two Jakes." *Washington Post*, August 10, 1990.

Kael, Pauline. "Prizzi's Honor." *New Yorker*, June 1985.

Maslin, Janet. "The Crossing Guard." *New York Times*, November 15, 1995.

Maslin, Janet. "Ironweed." *New York Times*, December 18, 1987.

Maslin, Janet. "The Shining." *New York Times*, May 23, 1980.

Maslin, Janet. "Terms of Endearment." *New York Times*, November 23, 1983.

Maslin, Janet. "The Witches of Eastwick." *New York Times*, June 12, 1987.

Mitchell, Elvis. "Anger Management." *New York Times*, April 11, 2003.

Orr, Christopher. "Something's Gotta Give." *Atlantic*, May 4, 2004.

Rainer, Peter. "About Schmidt." *New York*, December 16, 2002.

Staff writer. "The Raven." *Independent Exhibitor's Film Bulletin*, February 4, 1963.

Variety staff. "Goin' South." *Variety*, October 6, 1978.

Variety staff. "Head." *Variety*, November 6, 1968.

Variety staff. "The Raven." *Variety*, January 31, 1963.

ONLINE

Berardinelli, James. "Chinatown (United States, 1974)." ReelViews movie reviews website. http://www.reelviews.net/reelviews/chinatown.

Censored Films and Television at University of Virginia Library online. http://explore.lib.virginia.edu/exhibits/show/censored/walkthrough/film2.

Carr, Jay. "Five Easy Pieces." Turner Classic Movies. www.tcm.com.

Ebert, Roger. "The Departed." Great Movies page at RogerEbert.com, July 5, 2007.

Ebert, Roger. "Five Easy Pieces." Great Movies page at RogerEbert.com, March 16, 2003.

Horowitz, Josh. "Jack Nicholson Talks!" MTV.com, November 5, 2007.

Internet Movie Database. www.imdb.com.

The Last Detail (1973) financial information. The Numbers. http://www.the-num bers.com/movie/Last-Detail-The#tab=news.

Murray, Rebecca. "Diane Keaton Interview." About.com.

Murray, Rebecca. "Jack Nicholson Interview." About.com.

"Pledge, The: Interview with Jack Nicholson." Cinema.com. http://cinema.com/articles/601/pledge-the-interview-with-jack-nicholson.phtml.

Reeves, Carson. "Chinatown: Best Screenplay Ever?" *ScriptShadow* (blog), February 17, 2011. http://scriptshadow.blogspot.com/2011/02/chinatown-best -screenplay-ever.html.

Smith, Richard Harlan. "The Terror." Turner Classic Movies. www.tcm.com.

Smithey, Cole. "Leonardo DiCaprio Interview." ColeSmithey.com, October 11, 2006.

Sobczynski, Peter. "Existential Westerns: Criterion Editions of 'The Shooting,' 'Ride in the Whirlwind.'" RogerEbert.com, November 26, 2014.

The Teacher: The Memoir of Blacklisted Actor and Teacher to the Stars, Jeff Corey. Michelle Cohen Projects. http://www.michellecohenprojects.com.

FILMS

Note: All films listed herein were screened from the DVD and Blu-ray sources cited in the chapter credit boxes.

Making "The Shining" (1980). Directed by Vivian Kubrick.

TELEVISION

"Burt Reynolds Discusses His Career in Showbiz." *Larry King Live*, February 23, 2000.

Horowitz, Josh. "Jack Nicholson 'Furious.'" *MTV News*, November 6, 2007.

INDEX

ABOUT THE AUTHOR

James L. Neibaur is a film historian whose books include *Early Charlie Chaplin*, *Buster Keaton's Silent Shorts* (with Terri Niemi), *The Elvis Movies*, *The James Cagney Films of the 1930s*, *The Clint Eastwood Westerns*, and *The Essential Mickey Rooney*. He has also written hundreds of articles, reviews, and essays, including over forty entries in the *Encyclopedia Britannica*.